D1114891

WISE
MIND
LIVING

WISE
MIND
LIVING

MASTER YOUR EMOTIONS, TRANSFORM YOUR LIFE

Erin Olivo PhD

sounds true
BOULDER, COLORADO

Sounds True
Boulder, CO 80306

© 2014 Erin Olivo

Sounds True is a trademark of Sounds True, Inc.
All rights reserved. No part of this book may be used or reproduced in any manner
without written permission from the author(s) and publisher.

Published 2014

Cover design by Rachael Murray
Book design by Beth Skelley

Printed in the United States of America

Library of Congress Cataloging-in-Publication Data
Olivo, Erin.
  Wise mind living : master your emotions, transform your life / Erin Olivo, PhD.
    pages cm
  Includes bibliographical references.
  ISBN 978-1-62203-245-7 (alk. paper)
  1. Emotions. 2. Change (Psychology) I. Title.
  BF531.O45 2014
  152.4—dc23

                                    2014010445

Ebook ISBN 978-1-62203-383-6

10 9 8 7 6 5 4 3 2 1

This book is dedicated to my patients,
who inspire me each and every day with the
courage and vulnerability they bring to the process of therapy.
They show me that transformation truly is possible.
I am honored to be a part of their lives.

Contents

Acknowledgments

I am so grateful to the many people who helped make this book a reality, supporting and encouraging me and sharing their wisdom throughout the process.

First and foremost, I want to thank my mentor, Mehmet Oz, for his ongoing guidance and friendship. This book literally would not exist if not for his wise counsel and generosity. It was a specific conversation with him that inspired me to become an author and set this book in motion, and many conversations since have helped bring it to fruition.

I am also profoundly grateful for two incredible women who helped me every step of the way. Colleen Kapklein's wonderful writing and organizational talents made this a better book, and working with her made the writing process so much more enjoyable. Deborah Strafella's tenacity, great taste, and commitment to always creating something excellent constantly amaze me, and I am so grateful for her friendship and collaboration.

I couldn't have a found a better home for this book than at Sounds True. I offer my sincerest thanks to everyone in the Sounds True family for their unwavering support. I want to specifically thank Tami Simon for her visionary leadership, Nancy Smith for her nurturing presence, Haven Iverson and Leslie Brown for their invaluable guidance, and Mitchell Klute for his insightful direction of my audio book.

I am very fortunate to have been taught by many wise and inspiring mentors throughout my career. I am indebted to Marsha Linehan, whose groundbreaking work provides the foundation for how I practice as a psychotherapist and how I teach Wise Mind Living. I am deeply grateful for the guidance of my former professors and supervisors Kim Lehnert, Christine Foertsch, Lisa Miller, Xavier Amador, and Richard Sloan. For my introduction to and ever-evolving understanding of spiritual and contemplative practice, I remain forever indebted to the wisdom and teachings of Robert Thurman, Joseph Loizzo, and Jon Kabat-Zinn.

I am also incredibly lucky to have an amazing group of colleagues and friends who assist and collaborate with me in my clinical practice and who buoyed me through the challenges of writing this book. My deepest thanks to Julie Nathan, Cecilia Dintino, Hannah Starobin, Gina Pulice, and Mark Wilson for helping me live and practice in Wise Mind, and to my dear friends Katherine Johnson, Stephanie Martin, Rachel Gotler, and Melissa Stewart for being there with reassurance and practical support during moments of Emotion Mind.

My parents were the first people to show me what Wise Mind Living truly means, and they introduced me to the concepts of dialectical behavior therapy without even knowing it. I am so deeply grateful that from the very beginning of my life they taught me how to acknowledge, honor, and master my emotions. They did so both directly and by the example they set in how they live their lives. I wouldn't be who I am without their love, wisdom and firm foundation.

And lastly, I want to thank my husband and my son for the joy and meaning they bring to my life, and for showing me the full scope and magnitude the emotion of love can reach! I love you both more than I ever dreamed was possible.

1

WISE MIND VS. EMOTION MIND

Stress, Emotions, Health, and Happiness

So, how *are* you? If I had to guess your answer, I'd go with, "I'm so stressed out!" You might even feel like your stress is never ending; I hear this from new patients all the time. When they describe what is going wrong for them, they refer to it as stress. But by that, they could mean they're experiencing a bad mood, aches and pains, relationship conflict, or pretty much anything that simply is not going their way. Or they might be referring to overscheduling, overspending, or overexercising. Or *lack* of exercise or sleep. Or eating too much. Or not eating enough. "I'm so stressed out!" might reflect an inability to say no or a major life transition or serious trauma. Or a microtrauma ("I forgot my lunch!").

No matter what is going on with us, we tend to think of ourselves as being under stress. And so we are. But it's not the stress per se that we most need to deal with to improve our lives. These days, we can't wade two inches deep into the media without being splashed with advice on how to beat, reduce, or avoid stress—as if that were the very thing we need in order to find happiness, reach our full potential, or otherwise live the lives we dream of. "If only I could get rid of this *stress*!"

We live in a culture that is very efficient at generating stressors (thanks, smartphone) and that, at the same time, makes stress reduction seem like an urgent task at which we are all failing to measure up. The way we think about stress stresses us out! But when we identify stress as our main problem in this way, when we target stress busting as the way to improve our lives, we make a fundamental error in thinking. If we only focus on the stress that our problems are causing or on the problems themselves, nothing will change. If we really want to make a difference for ourselves and our health, if we want to free ourselves from our "issues," whatever they may be, we need to focus our attention on the *emotions* underlying these problems. These emotions—unmanaged and unmastered—are not only causing the problems; they are also creating the stress.

If we want to manage our stress, we have to manage our emotions. If we want to manage our *lives*, we have to manage our emotions!

Our stress and our problems both stem from emotions that are being overlooked, ignored, denied, misunderstood, misinterpreted, suppressed, or just generally poorly handled. We might pin the blame on the boss or our kids, on having too little time or too much to do, or on any number of other things. But underneath that, the real troublemakers are our *feelings* about those things and how we manage those feelings. Our distressing emotions, when they aren't being taken care of in a productive way, are at the root of all of our most common issues, including overeating, chronic relationship conflict, money mismanagement, substance abuse, and even, in many cases, poor physical health.

So, as you can see, when you get a handle on your emotions, you'll get a handle on your problems—and your stress. Then you will be able to effect a top-to-bottom change in every aspect of your life through the choices you make every day: *master your emotions—transform your life.*

LIVING IN WISE MIND
Tara Is Really Stressing

Tara thought her life had been pretty well transformed already when she gave birth to her daughter. She wasn't really in the market for any more big changes, thank you very much. But the baby was two months old now, and Tara was "really stressing" about whether she should go back to work. She was lucky enough to have three months of maternity leave from her teaching job, but she was down to the last few weeks of it, and the school was expecting her back. If only she could get some sleep, Tara told me, maybe she wouldn't be freaking out about this; but it seemed like it was all she could think about. How could she go back to a class full of chemistry students when she was nursing her baby every two hours? How could she leave her tiny, precious daughter in the hands of those *strangers* at the day-care center?

But how could she not go back to the job she loved? How could she just abandon her students midyear? Also, would her daughter *ever* stop spitting up? Tara said she thought she no longer owned a single piece of clothing that wasn't stained with baby "urp." What was she going to wear to work, anyway? And what if her daughter learned to walk while Tara was at work? That's what happened to her friend Mindy, who was texted a photo of her son's first steps. But if Tara took a year off—or two or three—so she wouldn't miss things like that, would she ever be able to get back in a classroom? And what if she found that she hated being at home? Her other friend Yvonne had quit her job when her baby was born, only to go stir-crazy and start job hunting before her kid learned to walk. It was all too much stress, Tara told me, and she just didn't know what to do.

But before Tara could figure out what to do, she needed to figure out what she was feeling, down underneath the stress. What emotions were generating that stress? Until she could answer that question, she would be stuck feeling out of control. ◑

As Tara was about to find out, and as you will see, emotions drive the decisions you make, the actions you take, what you think, and, yes, how you feel. As long as *you* have your hands on the wheel, you'll have a good trip: your emotions will alert you to obstacles and speed you where you want to go. But if you're not steering—or, like Tara, if you don't quite realize you need to steer—if you take your eyes off the road, if you leave your emotions to their own devices to take you wherever *they're* headed, then you're going to crash. Or at the very least, you'll end up somewhere other than where *you* set out to go.

WISE MIND LIVING

The scenario with *you* driving rather than your emotions driving is one I describe to my patients as living in Wise Mind. If your emotions are running things, you're in Emotion Mind. At the other end of the spectrum, when you are doing your best impersonation of Mr. Spock, you are in Logic Mind. Wise Mind Living is when you sustain a mind-set that balances emotion and logic. You really don't want Mr. Spock driving either: just as Emotion Mind runs too hot, Logic Mind runs too cool. Wise Mind, then, is Goldilocks's *juuuuust* right. Wise Mind proceeds logically but includes emotional information. It embraces both the rationality of Logic Mind *and* the sensitivity of Emotion Mind. It is practical and intuitive, rule based and flexible. It both protects your self-interest and takes others into account.

Imagine for a moment that you're car shopping. If you've had a terrible fight with your spouse or, at the other end of the spectrum, if you closed a really big deal at work, and you get really amped up one way or the other—all *before* you hit the dealership—then you are fully immersed in Emotion Mind. You might come home with that totally awesome sports car. Who cares if there's nowhere to put the car seat or stow the groceries? You totally deserve it! Did you check out how fast this thing goes!? And how about the color? Everyone is going to be able to see this car coming!

But what if Logic Mind were your shopping assistant? You could research the safest, most fuel-efficient car available, with the highest-rated everything right down to the cup holders, and then track down the absolute best price available. In fact, you could spend so much time figuring out the ideal car that you might never get around to buying an actual car. Or you might end up with the world's most egregiously unattractive vehicle (it had a lot of fans at *Effective Engineering* magazine), in an . . . interesting . . . shade of mustard (and it wasn't one penny over your budget). Who cares if it is a bit depressing to look at? Who cares if the winter-weather antiskid device isn't strictly necessary here in Florida? Any intelligent person could see that this is the safest car and the smartest choice.

However, if you went shopping in Wise Mind, you'd bring home something that works for you, practically speaking, but also something that you enjoy driving. Like maybe a minivan . . . in cherry red. The one with really nice handling and a port for your iPod?

Living in Wise Mind (like shopping in Wise Mind) sets you up to make good choices. Choices that work for you. Choices that get you what you need. Choices you can live with. Choices that make you feel good. Choices that fit your life and your interpersonal situation. Choices that both optimize the good and minimize the bad. Choices that balance what you think and what you feel.

Emotion Mind usually leads to poor decisions, because you do not show up with your best self to handle whatever circumstances you find yourself in. Emotions can give you important information, but Emotion Mind often can't see anything beyond initial, visceral reactions, and it leaves no room for rationality.

Logic Mind, on the other hand, might let you make good rational sense, but it has a blind spot for how feelings affect a situation. Every situation has emotional content, and if you don't factor in that content, you can't win fairly because you won't be dealing from a full deck. With Logic Mind, you might make what looks like a smart choice on paper, but it won't be the best real-world choice.

Wise Mind and Emotion Mind are concepts developed by Marsha Linehan for the specialized type of therapy she developed known as dialectical behavior therapy (DBT). (So is Logic Mind, though she calls it Reasonable Mind.) I've come to use the phrase Wise Mind with my patients in a broader sense than its original DBT meaning. DBT is designed specifically to deal with truly extreme emotion; I more often tap into the power of Wise Mind to handle everyday emotion. Wise Mind Living braids together strands from a few therapeutic and philosophical traditions and refers to an overarching approach to life. Wise Mind Living is about optimizing mental, emotional, and physical well-being.

Wisdom is the supreme part of happiness.
SOPHOCLES

IT'S WHAT I TEACH AND WHAT I DO

Over the course of nineteen years of working with patients, I've relied on a combination of DBT, cognitive behavior therapy (CBT), mindfulness-based cognitive therapy, mind-body strategies (the ones with good research backing up their efficacy), and Buddhist philosophy and meditation practices to create an approach that I call Wise Mind Living. It's what I've studied, what I've trained in, and what I use in my own life. My expertise comes not just from formal education and professional experience but also from growing up, dating (is there another area with as many emotions that really need managing as dating?), getting married, building a business, and parenting—in other words, it comes from living my life. I know that what I teach my patients works because I've done it—and do it—myself.

Everyone struggles with emotions: you, me, the Dalai Lama, *everyone*. And it's not just the negative emotions—even love and happiness are emotional experiences that can benefit by being managed. That's how you wring every last drop of goodness out of them! Wise Mind is not just a state you access once in a while to deal with a panic attack here or a heartbreak there. It's also not just for problems. It's more like a zone you try to stay in as you live your everyday life—lessening the grip of Emotion Mind without getting stuck in Logic Mind to find the balanced Wise Mind state in between. Wise Mind is for issues big and small. It's for problems and opportunities. Every stage of life comes with its own challenges—emotional and otherwise—and Wise Mind can see you through them all. That's why I call it Wise Mind Living.

Anyone can live in Wise Mind as long as they are willing to learn a handful of straightforward skills and practical strategies and deploy them daily. If that is you, you will understand and manage your emotions, control the stress emotions can cause, and find a path out of negative behavior patterns that are both fueling and fueled by distressing emotions. Everyone has emotions, and they affect us all every day. Emotion guides what we feel, think, and do—*and so does Wise Mind*. Mastering your emotions with Wise Mind strategies calms your body and physical symptoms, shapes thought patterns that help rather than hinder you, and supports productive action rather than uncontrolled *reaction*.

The principles of Wise Mind Living can work like therapy, or as a part of therapy, but they are just as useful for people who haven't felt any need for therapy. Wise Mind Living is good for everyone, because everyone has emotions. You don't have to be intensively struggling with those emotions to benefit from Wise Mind Living. Living in Wise Mind can help you get out of a jam, but it's even better for keeping you out of sticky messes in the first place.

LIVING IN WISE MIND
Tara Gets Wise

After becoming a mother, Tara spent a lot of time in Emotion Mind, pinging from one overwhelming idea to the next: "I don't know what I'm doing! Is it supposed to be like this? I can't cope with this! Will she ever stop crying? How can he sleep through this? I want my life back!" It's not unusual for a new phase of life to come with new emotional challenges. Even someone like Tara, who'd felt she had it pretty much together, can be thrown for a loop. And she was particularly vulnerable because of the physical challenges of new motherhood; getting by on next-to-no sleep, for example, was priming her to take everything harder than she otherwise might.

Of course, Tara didn't know about Emotion Mind when she first sought help. So her first step was the same as it is for almost all of my patients: getting familiar with the concept of Emotion Mind and learning to identify when it was happening to her. Tara's second step was to identify which emotion, exactly, was pushing her around. That required a bit more work, but as she went through it, Tara came to see that she was fearful of what her principal—and her husband—would think of her. But Tara also felt guilty, both when she thought about anyone else caring for her daughter *and* when she imagined her students permanently stranded with a sub. For the trifecta, Tara also realized she felt sad at the prospect of missing time with her daughter, with simultaneous feelings of sadness at the prospect of not teaching.

Tara had already tried to work out a stress-busting solution with a strategy that had always worked for her before: she made a list of pros and cons.

She analyzed her choices to within an inch of her life. The money she'd lose in salary. The money they'd save on day care. The statistics on getting another teaching job after gaps of varying lengths. The outcome data on kids in day care. And on and on. She summoned the full (and considerable) power of her Logic Mind, yet still somehow, she couldn't get everything to add up to an answer. There was no column in her spreadsheet for emotion, and without it, her equations were never going to balance.

Swinging as she was between Emotion Mind and Logic Mind, Tara was poised to find her balance in Wise Mind. She had three conflicting emotions to contend with, so she learned to step back from them enough to observe her emotions, describing them and their effects to herself, then reality-testing them. These were her feelings—no one could deny that—but was she thinking about them in ways that worked for her? How would she know if her actions were good choices? What was she going to do about how she felt?

Tara would find her answers with Wise Mind. She would find a way to honor her personal and professional self, her husband and her baby, her job and her life. Her thoughts about the political implications of her choice, her calculations about her financial future, and her long-standing commitment to education would all be factored in, and so would her sudden fascination with baby booties, her mixed feelings about being a full-time caregiver, and her full-to-overflowing supply of mother's love. ⦿

 WISE MIND LIVING PRACTICE
Catch Yourself in Emotion Mind

Now that you know about Emotion Mind, Logic Mind, and Wise Mind, try catching yourself in the midst of each one. Start with Emotion Mind. Can you recognize when your emotions are driving solo?

EMOTIONS 101: THE OWNER'S MANUAL AND TOOL KIT

Wise Mind Living is like Emotions 101. Wait, I take that back: Emotions 101 sounds like a college-level course, and that is more or less what

I aimed to give Tara, as I do all my patients. But the fact is, I wish everyone were taught these skills earlier in school, right alongside learning to read and count. Even sooner, really. In fact, I'm doing my best to raise my son to know these things, and he's only just started preschool. Any parent could do the same. I am often amazed at the way my son's young mind takes to this so naturally, unlike the adults in my practice and my life, who not only have to learn new ways of being but also have to let go of some ingrained habits that are not serving them well.

For the record, Wise Mind Living does *not* involve rummaging around in any baggage you may be carrying (though it does aim to lighten the load). Living in Wise Mind is about dealing with your emotions *now*—what they are in the present, how they affect you today, and how they show up in your behavior. Wise Mind Living is focused on solutions; it is about doing what works, right now.

Tara has come to think of Wise Mind Living as a combination owner's manual and tool kit for her emotions. It provides information and tools for maintaining emotions for optimum efficiency and peak performance. It gives solutions for when she breaks down. It lets her know what the warning lights look like, what they mean, and what she needs to do when she notices them. And it explains the basics about what emotions are, how they work, and what good they do.

If you intend to drive, rather than letting your emotions chart your course, it's wise to be familiar with the contents of the owner's manual and to be prepared with the right tools. It'll help you be the best driver you can be and ensure a smooth, safe trip.

CHANGE

When the trip is rocky, when you don't like the way you are feeling and don't want to feel that way, Wise Mind Living can help you change, or manage, that emotion—even when you can't change the circumstances! This is exactly the promise I made to Tara. Figuring out how to change your emotions, or their intensity, will also allow you to change the behavior problems (overeating, overspending, and so on) that those emotions produce when left unmanaged. In Tara's case, the problem was paralyzed decision making.

The process of change begins with understanding what emotions are, how they work, and how they serve you. Wise Mind strategies helped Tara recognize and accurately identify the emotions she was feeling as she was feeling them, including what she felt physically. Wise Mind helped her be equally aware of her reactions to her emotions—that is, how she was thinking about them and what she was doing. Once she was tuned in in all these ways—and *only* when she was tuned in in all these ways—was she able to *change* how she felt, what she thought, and what she did. In the end, Tara decided not to go back to full-time teaching right away; instead, she got a flexible job tutoring students who miss school for long stretches due to medical reasons. Finding and using her Wise Mind, Tara was able to reduce her vulnerability to distressing emotions and increase her experience of positive ones, both as she planned her future and as she lived her plan. She decreased her emotional suffering, let go of painful emotions, and relieved stress. Just as she did, you too can choose constructive thought and behavior patterns. You can ease any physical symptoms and even improve your long-term health, both physical and mental.

However you feel right now, with Wise Mind Living, *you can feel better*.

WHEN YOU CAN'T CHANGE

Strategies for change are only half of the Wise Mind tool kit, because, of course, there are some things you can't change. (Just ask Tara. No matter how she looked at it, the fact remained that she simply was not going to be able to teach full-time *and* care for her daughter full-time.) Although you are in charge of more than you might think when it comes to what you can change, you will also experience irresistible forces and immovable objects, just like everyone else does. The trick is to simultaneously be ready, willing, and able to change *and* accept what you cannot change: that very balance is Wise Mind Living. Tara had to make her choice *and* come to grips with being unable to do two things at once.

Wise Mind strategies help you learn to abide the negative effects of what you can't change and to cope with them, without allowing them to push you into destructive behavior. Wise Mind represents a more philosophical level of acceptance, one at which you really stop resisting something and simply let it be. When you do, you will find that much of your suffering has come from engaging in an impossible struggle. Acceptance is often the path that takes you away from the issues that regularly trip you up—whether they involve food, money, addiction, toxic relationships, or anything else—and toward stability, fulfillment, and the elusive state of "happiness." Wise Mind strategies help you reach acceptance, while skirting passivity and defeatism.

LEARN. LIVE. REPEAT.

The two kinds of strategies you draw on to experience Wise Mind Living are change strategies and acceptance strategies. The change category involves calming your body, changing how you think, and changing how you act, which chapters 6, 7, and 8 explain in more detail. Acceptance strategies include mindfulness, observing your emotion, coping, and specific acceptance skills, which you'll learn more about in chapters 2, 4, and 9, only one of which is specifically about acceptance. A big chunk of acceptance is actually awareness, or learning to understand emotion and your emotions, which is what chapters 3 and 5 are all about.

The trick with Wise Mind is that you usually have to use many—or even all—of these skills at once. But you can't learn the strategies the same way you use them; you have to take them in one at a time. So I hope you'll be patient with yourself, and with me, as we begin layering in the different components. Each is valuable in and of itself, but it's not until you reach the point where you can click them all in place together that you'll experience the full potential of Wise Mind Living. As you pick up each new piece, you'll be able to understand more about the others that you've already put in place. Putting together all these building blocks is the way Tara figured out how she wanted to handle her work/life balance.

I'll suggest to you the same thing I suggested to Tara—it's the advice I give to all my patients: Look at your approach to Wise Mind Living as being made up of two phases. During the first phase, you're in it to *learn* it; in the second phase, you *live* it. You can use this book in basically that way: reading the first nine chapters takes you through the learning phase; following the Wise Mind Living program (chapter 10) is the living phase. Here's a preview of some of the major strategies you will learn and then live.

Mindfulness

Mindfulness, the topic of the next chapter, comes first because you simply can't live in Wise Mind without it. Mindfulness is a way of focusing your attention on just the here and now—really *noticing* the present moment—and regarding what you find there without judgment. Mindfulness is a multipurpose tool, and you'll use it in lots of ways in Wise Mind Living. One of my favorites—and often the first one I teach a new patient—is the body scan (see "Wise Mind Living Practice: Mindfulness Body Scan," page 29). Later, you will use mindfulness to tune in not just to your body but also to your thoughts and your emotions themselves. In advanced forms, you'll practice mindfulness of what you do as you are doing it—essentially, the mindfulness of *being*. Mindfulness, as you will learn, is absolutely key to acceptance.

The Language of Emotion

A second acceptance strategy brings together the key pieces of how you understand emotion in general and your emotions specifically. Together, these two pieces give you a language of emotion; becoming fluent in this language is crucial to reaching Wise Mind. Getting a grip on how emotions work, how to accurately identify and label emotions, and what purposes emotions serve allows you to be in charge of your emotions, rather than having your emotions controlling you. The practice you've already learned of catching yourself in Emotion Mind (see "Wise Mind Living Practice: Catch Yourself in Emotion Mind," page 8) is the most basic entryway into using the language of emotion to your advantage. It's what made the biggest immediate difference to Tara, and it's likely to be just as enlightening for you—*enlightening* not only as in, it will give you understanding, but also as in, it will lighten your load!

Sit with Your Emotions

Many of my patients balk at this third strategy. When I direct them to sit with their emotions as a homework assignment, they fix me with a look that says, "You want me to *what?*!" It rarely strikes anyone as a good idea to just sit still and feel—really and fully feel—an emotion that's causing grief. In fact, a lot of people have devoted quite a lot of energy to *not* feeling those emotions, whether they have done so consciously or unconsciously. But this is the crux of Wise Mind Living: to master your emotions, you must learn to simply experience them. I promise you that, ultimately, you will be glad you did. Allowing yourself to feel the full force of an emotion is freeing. Everyone survives the experience, and there's something powerful in that alone, because you know at a very basic level that you *can* handle it.

Sitting with your emotions is also a part of how you work with them, which is why many of the Wise Mind Living exercises begin by sitting with an emotion. And you won't be unprepared to go into really feeling what you feel, because mindfulness and understanding emotions both support you in the endeavor, as does calming your body (see the next section). Bringing all of these skills to bear so you can *be* with your emotions for a while is what sets you up for changing what you feel if you don't like it. Then you'll be able to respond rather than just react. You'll be ready for strategies for change that target your thoughts, feelings, and behavior and be able to practice acceptance when you're facing something you can't change.

Calm Your Body

Calming your body is always the first of the change strategies. It is a good way to ready yourself to use acceptance strategies. It may also be a by-product of acceptance practices, especially mindfulness. Relieving any physical symptoms of distressing emotions prepares you to learn, think clearly, solve problems, and use any other available strategies, without your energy and attention being unduly distracted or divided.

Another important benefit of calming your body is that it gives you an opportunity to listen to your body. Your physical sensations are a gold mine that can give you a lot of information about your emotions. How you feel *physically* is a kind of map of how you feel *emotionally*.

Guided relaxation is a typical way to calm your body. Maybe you've already tried one of those CDs that features a soothing voice talking you through getting comfortable, closing your eyes, and imagining yourself lying on the beach listening to the waves, or picturing a flickering candle. Chapter 6 offers several exercises for calming your body (see pages 89–92). You have a choice of how you want to begin down the path of change—the path that also includes changing your thoughts and your actions.

WHAT HAPPINESS LOOKS LIKE

In learning how to manage your emotions, you can leave behind the damaging or unproductive ways you may have been dealing—or not dealing—with them. When you identify and acknowledge what you are feeling rather than burying or ignoring it, when you untangle your big ball of stress so you can see plainly the emotions that are caught up in there, you can actually *lose* that stress, not just relieve it. Stress is just a symptom—a symptom you can't get rid of without addressing the underlying issue. Living in Wise Mind, you eliminate the symptom by treating the cause at the source. With Wise Mind, you aim for bigger than a bandage or an aspirin; instead, you're going for lasting solutions and sustainable, positive change.

Changing your relationship with your emotions will change all of your relationships (with food, money, friends, family, and all the rest). In fact, mastering your emotions is the *only* path to permanently resolving weight, interpersonal, financial, or other issues. You can diet all you like, for example, or exercise like a maniac every day, but if you don't deal with the emotions underlying your struggles with food or weight, your results are going to be cosmetic at best—and always temporary. If you master your emotions, you will be able to tell a very different story—one in which emotions won't stress you so much anymore—and you'll have new strategies for constructively handling any emotions or stress, so you won't default to problematic behaviors when under pressure.

Managing emotions does not come naturally to everyone, but it is a skill anyone can learn. And as with any skill, mastering your emotions takes practice; the more you practice, the easier it becomes, and the better at it you'll get. *Wise Mind Living* guides you through all the specific skills that go into living in Wise Mind. It details a program that focuses on the here and now and on what you are doing (or not doing) and what is working (or not working). If you commit to following the Wise Mind Living program outlined in chapter 10, then by the end of six weeks, you will experience relief from whatever the primary driving force was that made you pick up this book in the first place. You'll be armed with the tools you need to productively address any distressing emotions and the negative behavior patterns they can inspire, to prevent or tame any resulting stress, and—this is key—to enjoy the full force of positive emotions.

Learning to live in Wise Mind is the path to physical and mental well-being and a balanced and meaningful life. This is what happiness looks like.

2

MINDFULNESS

The Wisdom of Being
in the Present Moment

L iving in Wise Mind is about managing your emotions. To manage
your emotions, you need to pay attention to your emotions. To
pay attention to your emotions, you need to pay attention to your
experience. To pay attention to your experience, you need to know how
to pay attention, period. That's all mindfulness is, really: paying attention. And managing your emotions means simply treating them with
mindful attention. This is why this chapter begins with what mindfulness is and how you can do it.

Mindfulness is paying attention to whatever is happening moment by
moment, without being judgmental. It means waking up to your experience in the present moment and not thinking about the past or the
future. As with anything else, to get the hang of it, you have to practice.
You can (and will) use mindfulness in a lot of forms, in a lot of ways, but
the first goal, for our purposes, is simply to learn how to control your
focus and attention. Attention can be a really powerful tool for managing your emotions, but only when you are in charge of it.

So many of us humans tend to go through our days on autopilot,
which is essentially the opposite of mindfulness. We act unconsciously
or habitually, even forming thoughts and judgments without conscious
awareness of what we are doing (or why or how well). We just react. We
spend most of our energy rehashing the past or rehearsing the future:

wishing, hoping, planning, ruminating, missing, regretting. We are disconnected from what is happening in our lives—right now, in the present moment—and even within our own bodies and minds. In this mode, emotions seem to just sort of happen to us, and we might not acknowledge them, understand them, or realize we can control them. Or we might try to dodge emotions or shut them out. Either way, this is a recipe for emotion to overwhelm us. When we are not in the moment, we don't actually feel our feelings, and that creates *more* of the very emotions we may wish to avoid. It also doesn't (and can't!) solve the problems we are trying to escape.

We can make another choice, however. We can switch off the autopilot and take the wheel ourselves. This starts with mindfulness. Anyone can do it, even those whose usual M.O. is a far cry from mindful. Mindfulness is a skill like any other, so it can be learned. Also like any other skill, the more you practice it, the better you will get at it.

Plenty of people have written plenty of books on mindfulness—I have a bookmark in a lovely book on my bedside table right now, as I almost always do—and if you ask me, the more you learn about mindfulness, the more you'll get out of it. Still, mindfulness is just one tool in your Wise Mind Living toolbox: the most important tool, perhaps, but still not a solo act. So I'm going to give you a very targeted introduction and show you how to start practicing mindfulness. You'll find that learning by doing is the way to go with mindfulness, as it's a lot harder to understand without trying it.

THE TWO-WORD GUIDE TO PRACTICING MINDFULNESS

For Wise Mind Living purposes, mindfulness is mainly about controlling your attention: directing it where you want it to go, redirecting it as necessary, then redirecting it again . . . and again. It's the skill in redirecting your focus that you're really after.

So here's the two-word guide on how to practice mindfulness: *pay attention.*

And I mean really pay attention. To things as they are. In the present moment.

And that's it.

Well, of course there's more (see the multitude of books already devoted to the subject). But in a nutshell, that's really what you need to know. Being mindful means summoning awareness and attention and deploying them inwardly and outwardly, with intention and compassion and without analysis or judgment. Notice all that is happening within your mind and body and in the world around you *right now*. Attending to one thing at a time, acknowledge, observe, and accept each sensation, experience, thought, and feeling as it arises, moment to moment.

Mindfulness means maintaining an attitude of *not doing*. As you begin to practice mindfulness, the whole point is to not seek to change anything; the goal is to not have a goal. This can take quite an adjustment for many people, especially those on a quest for a solution to a problem. That's precisely when most people urgently want to *do something*. The effectiveness of mindfulness, however, comes from not doing anything, not striving for anything other than simple awareness of the present moment. Sometimes this leads to a pleasant state of relaxation; sometimes it leads to an intense "in the zone" experience; and sometimes it involves *un*pleasant feelings. Whatever happens, your job is to simply note what comes your way—not judging, but accepting. The doing/ changing part will come, but it is not where you begin.

THE ONE-WORD GUIDE TO PRACTICING MINDFULNESS

The word is: *breathe.*

When you practice mindfulness, a common technique is to use your breath as an anchor—a way to stabilize your focus. You can use breathing as a practice in and of itself (see "Wise Mind Living Practice: Mindfulness of Breath," page 26). In almost every case, you'll begin and end a practice with your breath—to get your mind settled and ready for mindfulness and then again as a transition back out of practice. In addition, within many practices, you may find it helpful to use your breath as follows: As you breathe out, relax and release any tension or distraction you are experiencing. Then, as you breathe in, sharpen the focus on your attention.

THE MANY USES AND BENEFITS
OF MINDFULNESS

When it's first described, mindfulness can appear so simple that it hardly seems like a technique at all. But mindfulness is many layered, and once you try it, its power is unmistakable. It's also quite practical. It'll come in handy in all kinds of ways. Mindfulness is meant to be practiced both sitting still in a calm, quiet space *and* in the daily riot of living your life. It's for use with the minutiae and the momentous. I talk to my patients about using mindfulness when stuck in traffic, when at their own wedding, when deciding whether to eat another cookie, when facing the death of a parent, when they pull out their credit card, and during just about everything in between.

Mindfulness is a multipurpose tool. You can use it to help you relax, deal effectively with stress, let go of painful emotions, identify habits of mind that aren't working for you, and become more aware of what you think, feel, and do and the ways in which you do (and don't) choose those thoughts, feelings, and actions. You can use mindfulness to gather information that will help you make decisions and form an intention about what you want to change. You can even use mindfulness to improve your health. Research has demonstrated that practicing mindfulness decreases anxiety, depression, and other forms of emotional distress. It can also lower the risk of heart disease and "adverse cardiac events" and relieve chronic pain.

When you really have the whole mindfulness thing down and have gotten better at observing yourself, you can extend the practice to help you manage your interactions with other people: romantic partners, children, siblings, friends, parents, colleagues. In its most advanced form, you can use mindfulness to tap into a sense of universal connectedness with all of humanity and all of the earth. For many people, this is a form of spiritual experience or a direct way of touching the meaning of life, whether or not they consider themselves spiritual.

Just paying attention is not the answer to all of life's problems, as there does come a time when you can and should act; but it is the best way I know to prepare to take on any challenges and to take them on effectively.

FORMAL AND INFORMAL MINDFULNESS

Three different kinds of mindfulness practice are key to Wise Mind Living. The first is a formal meditation practice, where you sit down for ten to fifteen minutes (or however much longer you wish) with the intention of being mindful. This is what you'll be doing in the Mindfulness of Breath (page 26) and Mindfulness of Sound (page 28) exercises. This is the best way to learn mindfulness; as you move on to more advanced practices, it is an important way to tap the full power of mindfulness.

The second kind of mindfulness practice is informal practice, which you do as you go about your day. The practice is to bring mindful attention to whatever ordinary activity you choose, such as taking a shower. You still have to do it with intention—you have to mean for this particular shower to be an exercise in mindfulness—but you do it as a part of daily life, not in a separate space and time set aside specially for it. (See "Wise Mind Living Practice: Informal Mindfulness 1" on page 31 and "Wise Mind Living Practice: Informal Mindfulness 2" on page 32.) This very valuable skill gives you experience with mindfulness that you'll need for more advanced practices specific to managing emotions.

The third kind of mindfulness is living with mindful awareness, which requires practicing mindfulness not by doing an exercise but by bringing it to—and using it throughout—your day. It's the logical extension of an informal practice. One day you're mindfully eating your breakfast, according to plan, or mindfully waiting for the elevator as a sort of homework assignment, and the next thing you know, mindfulness is an integral part of how you are in the world and how you move through your day.

Ideally, you will have both a formal and an informal mindfulness practice. Informal practices, like those in this chapter, are sometimes easier to fit into your day. You may rely on informal practice when you are at your busiest, when life just takes over, when you are most likely to let a formal sitting meditation practice go—which are exactly the times you most need to be mindful.

The value of having a formal practice is that it will make you better at an informal one. The more experience you have with formal mindfulness, the easier it will be for you to draw on mindfulness as part of your daily activities. The more miles you log with both formal and informal practices, the better you'll be able to bring mindful awareness to your day-to-day life, even in difficult, stressful, or emotional times.

FOCUS. OBSERVE. CONGRATULATIONS! YOU'RE BEING MINDFUL.

Beginners' mindfulness meditation, in a formal practice, is a two-part mission: to *focus* and to *observe*. This mission can take you pretty much anywhere, though the classic place to start is with your own breath (see "Wise Mind Living Practice: Mindfulness of Breath" on page 26). Another great option is to start with the Mindfulness of Sound exercise (page 28). Eventually, you will use formal mindfulness to specifically focus on and observe your thoughts and your emotions.

No matter what you choose to apply mindfulness to as a meditation practice, you'll need the same two skills:

Focus

Imagine your attention as a spotlight. Shine that spotlight on one point of focus: your breath, say, or the sounds around you. As you focus on and attend to your spotlit area, the rest of the landscape of your mind should appear dimmer, in the background. Try to hold your spotlight steady. If your spotlight drifts off point—and it will—gently refocus it again on the point you chose. If you find you're thinking about the crick in your neck or how much longer is left in your practice or what's next on your agenda, just notice that fact and then come back to your breath (or other point of focus) with no judgment about your attention having slid off. Losing focus is *not* a mindfulness fail; rather, it is the very opportunity you are looking for when you practice mindfulness—it is the chance to practice redirecting your attention.

Observe

Whatever your focus, your job is to simply notice everything about it. Take the moment apart and break it down into component parts.

Observe. What is it? What is it made of? What is it like? What is it doing? What is happening to it? Let your spotlight illuminate your experience, whatever it is, without judgment. You are observing, noticing, and acknowledging, not analyzing, criticizing, or otherwise evaluating. Your job is to neither become attached to nor push away any part of what you are observing. Don't get stuck on any one aspect or in any one moment, and don't deny any aspect either. If you are being mindful of sounds, for example, don't let the sound of that rattletrap air conditioner take and hold center stage. Hear it—that's observing—and then let your attention move on to what else you can hear (observe).

When you first begin learning this part of mindfulness, it can be useful to label what you are observing. Labeling your experience is a tool for focusing attention. It engages your thinking mind, giving it an anchor point and keeping it from running away with your mindfulness. Labeling also comes naturally to most people—putting language to our experience is what we humans do. In fact, at the outset, it may be almost impossible not to put words on your experience. But as you get more proficient, you won't need to. Think of when you first learned something complex, like how to drive a car. You probably talked yourself through your earliest driving practice: "Okay, now, checking my mirrors, putting on my signal, pulling into traffic, braking . . . ." By now, however, having logged a million miles or so behind the wheel, you no longer narrate all these steps to yourself. But at the point in the process when you most needed to focus on what you were doing, your natural inclination was to put words to what was happening as it was happening.

As you label what you notice while you practice mindfulness, opt for more general language—more like "I am noticing a sensation" or "I am noticing a sound," rather than "The itch on my foot is driving me crazy" or "That is one loud and annoying alarm." The words you choose for this stage matter. You want to be careful to label without judging. You want "just the facts, ma'am," in neutral language, all set in the present tense. If you sit down to practice mindfulness and begin by observing that very act, then it is better to label by saying, "The air is cool," rather than, "The air is too cool" (judgment), or, "That draft is going to give me a headache" (future tense).

You should also remember that labeling is like training wheels: handy at first, but designed to be done away with once you're ready to balance and roll on your own.

BEING MINDFUL OF NOT BEING MINDFUL

Modern life is chock-full of habits of mind that get in the way of mindfulness. Be on the lookout for them in your own life. Steering clear of them will be part of practicing mindfulness.

Here are some of the most common things that pull people out of mindfulness:

- Thinking about the past (literally taking you out of the moment)
- Thinking about the future (ditto)
- Multitasking
- Judging, analyzing, criticizing, or evaluating
- Attaching to thoughts or observations
- Pushing away thoughts or observations
- Having a lack of intention
- Having a lack of compassion
- Being in denial

 WISE MIND LIVING PRACTICE
Catch Yourself Being Judge-y

Judgment is one of the most common ways to pull yourself out of mindfulness. Whether you are judging your experience as good, bad, or ugly, it's an obstacle to being fully present in the moment.

And you do it all the time. Everyone does. The way to do it less—the way to not let judging interfere with your ability to be mindful—is to increase your awareness of when you are judging.

Try spending a few days noticing all the judgments you make throughout the day. About anything and everything: "What the hell is that lady wearing?" "Yuck, this food is gross!" "I should not be the one handling this!" Any time you catch yourself playing Judge Judy, notice it, label it as a judgment, and resist the temptation to judge yourself for being judgmental. Then try to tell yourself the same story but with neutral (nonjudgmental) language: "Her shirt is bright." "Oh, that is bitter." "I have a task that I do not like." With enough practice, you'll begin to make that kind of switch automatically—in mindfulness practice as well as in life.

LIVING IN WISE MIND
"I Never Got Past Four"

Anya, a meditation teacher I work with, had just gotten back from a weeklong silent retreat the day I ran into her. When I asked her how it was, she said, "It was great! I never got past four." I knew she was referring to a very basic meditation practice where you count slowly from zero to ten—and start over again any time you lose your way. But I was surprised that such an experienced meditator would spend a whole week on it—without ever getting to ten!—and then be standing in front of me exclaiming about how much she got out of the retreat.

There turned out to be more to the story, of course, centered on Anya's irrational dislike of another participant at the retreat. She struggled with feeling so much judgment of another person and with how distracting it was to her own practice. Her emotions were pulling her away from the mindful awareness she'd planned on nurturing for one whole precious week of vacation time. In the end, though, the challenge of dealing with this unwelcome irritation turned out to be a great way for Anya to practice mindfulness of her emotions, and she was grateful for the opportunity.

Anya's experience is a good example of how useful the most basic practices are, even for experts. But here's the moral of the story and what I most want you to take away: *everyone's* thoughts wander. There's no such thing as deciding to be mindful, plunking down for fifteen minutes, and retaining complete focus for the entire time—not for Anya, not for me, not for you. Focus drifts; that's part and parcel of what mindfulness *is*. The skill you want to develop is the ability to gently bring your focus back on target. As many times as you have to. Without judgment of yourself for only getting to four . . . *again.* ⊕

Like a Buddhist

No matter what mindfulness practice you are doing, you may want to begin and end it the way it is done in Buddhist tradition. Not because I think you should be a Buddhist, or even because I think you should meditate like a Buddhist, but because the Buddhist way of opening and closing a practice is psychologically astute. From the perspective of a behaviorist like me, it's important to set a goal or intention for yourself and then check on your progress. It is reinforcing and makes it more likely that you will actually get the benefit and that you'll do it again.

As you begin any practice, bring to mind the motivation for the practice. What do you intend to focus on, work on, practice, accomplish? "This is about understanding and mastering my emotions," you might say to yourself. Or, "I am calming my body."

As you close your practice, bring your focus back to your breath and body, acknowledging the effort you have put into taking care of yourself in this way. Whatever benefit you've received from the practice, whatever has been meaningful about it to you, mentally mark it on the path of your ongoing quest for well-being.

 WISE MIND LIVING PRACTICE
Mindfulness of Breath

Settle yourself comfortably in a calm spot. Set an intention for how long you plan to practice. Close your eyes or, if you prefer, choose an object on which to rest your gaze. You should be in a relaxed state before you begin to practice mindfulness. If you need an assist in getting relaxed, you can do a quick relaxation exercise (there are several in chapter 6), or you can use any relaxation technique or guided relaxation you like. Just taking a few slow breaths before you begin may do it.

When you are ready:

Focus on your breath. The inhale and the exhale. The pause in between. Is there a pause? Refocus as many times as you need to.

Observe your breath. Notice how deep or shallow your breathing is. Note how your chest rises and falls. Does your abdomen move, too? Are you breathing through your mouth or your nose? Does your breath feel easy or tight? None of these questions has a right answer, and there are no required questions. If other aspects of your breathing reveal themselves to you as you practice, well, then, that's what you notice.

You may want to label your breath by counting. Count each full cycle of breath as one unit. So "Inhale, exhale, one . . . Inhale, exhale, two . . . Inhale, exhale, three" and so on until you have counted ten breaths; then repeat. When you find that your focus has wandered, simply refocus on your breath and start over at one.

This exercise is *not* about changing your breath. Go ahead and count how long each breath lasts if you like—that's a good way to hold focus and another way to label the experience for yourself—but you're not aiming to inhale any specific number of times or increase the length of your exhale or any such thing. Yogis, save your *pranayama* for another time. In mindfulness of breath, you are not "supposed" to breathe deeply—or shallowly, for that matter—or in through your mouth and out through your nose or any variation thereon. (Though you most definitely should breathe both in and out. Repeatedly. Highly recommended.)

On the other hand, you might find that observing your breath (or anything else) does change it. So if turning your attention to your breath leads to a slowing of your breathing rate, don't judge it. Just notice it, and move on.

You'll get the most out of mindfulness if you use formal practice at least a couple times a week. If you can fit it in every day, even better. Five or ten or fifteen minutes are enough. It doesn't have to be a marathon.

See if you can commit to a regular practice for just three weeks. Then see how you like it, what you get from it, if you learn from it. Then make a new plan for your mindfulness practice going forward. Add in more sessions or cut back on how many you're doing. Lengthen or shorten each session. Do what works for you and your emotional life. What kind of practice makes sure you are in Wise Mind when you need to be?

 WISE MIND LIVING PRACTICE
Mindfulness of Sound

This version of mindfulness is another basic, foundational practice everyone should try. It's especially useful to some mindfulness beginners for whom Mindfulness of Breath is not a comfortable fit. Mindfulness of Sound is often an easier starting place for people with anxiety or body-image issues or for those who find, for whatever reason, that tuning in to something going on in their bodies is disconcerting rather than grounding.

This practice has another very handy benefit: it helps you get good at noticing sounds and then moving on, which is useful for any kind of meditation because the thing that most often breaks a meditator's concentration is sound. There's no such thing as a completely quiet environment in which to meditate; get to a quiet enough place and you'll still hear your own heartbeat. So practicing mindfulness of sound helps you learn how to move past those moments when you might otherwise be disrupted by the dishwasher starting a new cycle, the kids outside hollering at each other, or the jackhammering out on the street.

Mindfulness of Sound begins the same way as Mindfulness of Breath. Once you are settled, comfortable, and relaxed, bring your attention to all the sounds around you. Observe all the layers of what you can hear: the dog barking, street noises, birdcalls, the hum of the fridge. You should even—especially!—take in the things you might normally tune out. Sit still, be quiet, and *listen*. Listen for the spaces between the sounds, too—the sounds of silence. The tick of the clock, the whoosh of the air vents.

Don't get stuck on any one sound, especially if you are critical of it. The first few times you use this practice, you might want to try labeling what you observe ("A car alarm is going off"), but be careful not to judge ("That alarm is so annoying! When is that idiot going to turn off his alarm? I can't meditate with that racket going on!"). Simply label what you observe and move on. Don't get attached to a sound, either; don't get pulled into that conversation in the hallway so that you're listening to the specific words people are saying. Instead, take in the sound of it as a whole.

 WISE MIND LIVING PRACTICE
Mindfulness Body Scan

This exercise could take a minimum of ten minutes (and up to an hour, if you are so inclined). It often takes at least five minutes to quiet the mind and settle into the practice. If it takes you longer, be sure to spend at least a few minutes on the exercise once you are calm. Try performing this scan daily, each time at least long enough to really get comfortable doing it.

Begin by sitting or lying down, with your eyes closed. Make sure you are comfortable.

Become aware of your body. Notice your posture. Feel the weight of your body supported by the surface underneath you.

Bring attention to the natural flow of your breath (don't try to change or deepen it; just notice it, however it is right now). Follow the full cycle of breath, noticing the breath entering the body on the inhale, filling the lungs, and making its way out of the body on the exhale.

Staying with the breath, bring your attention to each part of your body in turn, moving from your feet to your head. Notice any sensations that arise (tension, temperature, tingling). Rest your attention on each body part for a few moments, exploring its entire surface and structure, becoming aware of the bones, skin, and muscles at each stop before directing your attention to the next spot.

Start with your toes, moving gradually to your arches, heels, ankles, shins, calves, knees, thighs, pelvis, and buttocks, each in turn . . . all the while noticing what you find there. Then move on to becoming aware of the entire back of the body, the spine, the shoulder blades; then the front of the body, including the abdomen, lungs, and rib cage. Notice the rise and fall of each breath, perhaps sensing the beating of the heart. Note the intimate connections between the systems of the body as you go.

Next move along the arms, then the hands, and then the fingers—noticing. Then the throat, jaw, tongue, face, forehead, and crown of the head.

Your attention will inevitably drift. When you notice that it has, simply pick up from wherever you left off. Or you can return to focusing on your breath for a few moments first and then continue the scan.

Thoughts or emotions may arise as you do this exercise. If they do, just notice them without judgment; then let them go as you return to the body scan.

When you've scanned your entire body, take a moment to feel the body as a whole. Return your attention to the breath. Notice any effects of this practice. Right now, in this moment, allow yourself to feel relaxed and complete.

 WISE MIND LIVING PRACTICE
Mindfulness of Thoughts and Feelings

In this practice, you focus your attention on the contents of your mind—your thoughts and feelings. In other formal mindfulness practices, your job has been to not allow your thoughts and feelings to pull your focus, but here, your thoughts and feelings *are* your focus.

Begin as usual, tuning in to your breath and body, coming to rest in a place of balanced awareness. When you are ready, allow your awareness to include your thinking. Simply acknowledge whatever is happening in your mind, right now, in the present moment. Do you notice any running commentary, judgments, planning thoughts, remembering, storytelling? Do you notice a theme to your thoughts? Worry? Self-criticism? Longing for something?

There's a difference between, for example, *being lost* in planning and *observing* your planning thoughts. Notice the difference, so you can leave the former behind in favor of the latter, at least for right now. Allow your thoughts to simply be present as they are, without either pushing them away or following them. Acknowledge them as just thoughts. If you find yourself getting pulled into thinking instead of simply being mindful of thoughts, take a moment and return your attention to your breath.

Next, allow your attention to move to the strongest emotion present in you. There is no need to find an emotion if there isn't one. Just allow yourself to be open to emotion if it is there. Label this feeling with a name and just allow it to be present. See if you can locate this feeling in your body; if so, notice your physical experience of it. When you are ready, return your focus to your breath. Allow yourself to go back and forth between focusing on your breath for a while and then on your emotion for a while. (If at any point you feel overwhelmed by emotion, shift to your breath until you feel better.)

> Drink your tea slowly and reverently, as if it is the axis on which the earth revolves—slowly, evenly, without rushing toward the future. Live the actual moment. Only this moment is life.
>
> THICH NHAT HANH

 WISE MIND LIVING PRACTICE
Informal Mindfulness 1

Choose one of your regular daily activities and make it a mindfulness exercise. All that's required is for you to *intend* that brushing your teeth or chopping the salad or doing the dishes will be a mindfulness practice. Perhaps you've heard the Zen saying "Chop wood, carry water." This is the central heating, indoor plumbing–era version of that saying.

Your mindfulness practice doesn't have to be a chore. A walk in the woods makes a great mindfulness practice. So does a walk down the block. Or ten minutes on the treadmill. Or listening to one song on the radio. Or knitting a few rows. Whatever ordinary pastime you choose, all you have to do is set your intention and then be present with the activity. What does doing the action you've chosen feel like, sound like, smell like? If you set out to mindfully make the coffee, you will *focus* on the process and *observe* ("the beans rattling in the bag, the water starting to run cooler, the smell of roasted coffee beans").

Whatever your activity, focus on it and then observe your experience. This may look slightly different depending on your chosen activity. You can pick whatever fits in your regular life, but these examples should give you the general idea:

- When you wake in the morning, before getting out of bed, notice your breathing; take a few slow, comfortable breaths. Be aware of how your body feels as you move from lying down to sitting up, from sitting up to standing, from standing to walking.
- Pay attention as you eat. Notice the smells, flavors, and textures of your food. Chew slowly and completely. Keep your mind on what's on your plate and in your mouth.
- When talking with another person, take a moment to simply listen, appreciating this person's experience of the world, even if (especially if) it is different from your own.
- Walk mindfully, consciously placing your attention on each foot as it connects with and leaves the ground.
- When you are waiting in line, feel your feet on the ground and notice how you are holding yourself.

 WISE MIND LIVING PRACTICE
Informal Mindfulness 2

Designate something as a signal for you to take a moment for mindfulness: the phone ringing, waiting for an elevator, stopping at a red light. Choose something you know will happen at least a couple of times in your day. When you get one of these reminders, take a moment to be mindful—focus on and observe your experience. Give yourself the assignment of taking slow breaths any time the phone sounds, and don't pick up until after the fourth ring. Or at the elevator, once you've pushed that button to call the car, really notice where you are, tune in to what's going on in your body, and just be present in your life until you hear the *ding* that means your ride has arrived. When you pull up to a stoplight, do a quick version of Mindfulness of Breath or Mindfulness of Sound until the light turns green.

LIVING MINDFULLY

The better you get at both informal and formal mindfulness, the better you get at everyday awareness and presence in your daily life, and the closer you move to no longer doing mindfulness exercises but to simply living mindfully. You'll bring all the skills you've honed, whether by sitting on a meditation pillow or concentrating on soaping up in the shower, and throw them all into living fully in the moment, whatever you are doing. You are not really thinking or doing—you are just *being*, and being with everything you've got. Some call it "being in the flow." You might also know it as "being in the zone."

In reality, you can't spend every second of your life "in the zone," but if you've ever been there, you know what it is like to be 100 percent present with whatever you are doing and 100 percent present in the moment. (And if you've been "zoned out," you've experienced basically the opposite of living mindfully.) Most people find these fully mindful times in athletic or creative pursuits—playing sports or playing or listening to music, to take just two examples. Another common way to find it is during sex—good sex, anyway! The kind of sex where you are *not* saying to yourself, "Why is he putting his hand *there*? How do I look? What should I do next?" but when you are lost in the moment, not thinking—you are just being and fully present.

Some of my patients and friends recall feeling so carried away while painting, so consumed by color and light and the motion of the brush-strokes, that they lost all track of time. Some tell me about tennis games in which they were firing on all cylinders, simply *there* for every shot, not anticipating a win or fearing a loss, but just *playing* like there was nothing else in the world but this one point of focus. Some have experienced it playing with their children, absorbed in their world and the bonds between them. But it could occur any time at all when you feel you are fully inhabiting the moment, having thrown your whole self in, being really alive to what's going on while it is happening. Nothing about these experiences is rote or routine or unaware. Many people say these are the peak experiences of their lives. So although these are not everyday happenings, as you practice mindfulness, you will get glimpses of it here and there, and you can expect more and longer-lasting experiences of it as you go along.

 WISE MIND LIVING PRACTICE
Just This Moment

As you find yourself getting better at being able to hold your spotlight of focus on your breath, body, sound, thoughts, or emotions, you're ready to expand your field of awareness to include whatever comes up in the moment. In this exercise, you don't choose anything in particular to focus on; you simply stay open to, and aware of, whatever unfolds in each moment.

To begin this exercise, simply sit still and focus on your body and breath to ground yourself in *you*. As a kind of warm-up, focus for a while on your body, then on sound, then on thoughts and feelings. Then, when you are feeling centered and grounded and your spotlight is steady, focus it on *just this moment*. With no particular object of attention, open your awareness to everything happening in the moment: breath, sound, body sensations, thoughts, feelings, urges, emotions. Just notice what you observe, whatever is present for you, around you, or in you—whatever arises in the moment. You are essentially focusing on awareness itself. Don't follow thoughts or feelings, but don't push them away either. Simply let them come and go. The key, as with any mindfulness practice, is to remain nonjudgmental.

PUT UP YOUR TENT ON A SUNNY DAY

Living fully in the present moment can be a challenge even when you are feeling pretty good; trying to do so when you are upset is a tall order and is not for novices. As you are starting out, practice when you are feeling relatively calm. As they say in DBT, it's wiser to put up your new tent for the first time on a sunny day, because you don't really want to try to figure out its intricacies on a rainy night. On the other hand, in the middle of the storm is when you will most benefit from the shelter that your tent can provide. But it won't work if it leaks or blows away because you missed a bit here or installed something a bit backward there while trying to decipher the directions in the wet and dark.

In the same way, you will want to rely on mindfulness when the going gets tough, but that will only work best after you have a bit of fair-weather experience under your belt. Then, when the storm is raging, mindfulness will allow you to be the calm at the eye of it. You are not going to turn back the storm. You are not even going to try. But you are going to be aware of the storm, allowing it to move through, noting what is happening and what it feels like: "Huh, those are some serious winds. There's that lightning again. I am quite soaked." Until you try it, however, you will have to take my word for it—this kind of awareness is powerful in and of itself. We will get to strategies for coming in out of the rain and getting out of the path of the storm, but until then, let mindfulness be your umbrella.

MINDFULNESS AND YOUR EMOTIONS

Mindfulness is a beautiful and useful thing in and of itself. But it's covered here because you are going to put it to particular use to manage your emotions. Bringing mindful attention to your emotions helps you break them down and understand them (as you'll learn about more specifically in chapter 3). Mindfulness will enable you to work with your emotions, allow you to identify and make changes, and guide you in coming to acceptance when that is required. Mindfulness brings you to Wise Mind.

3

MIND YOUR BRAIN

The Cycle of Emotion

Emotions are produced by physiology, cognition, and behavior. So to understand emotions, you have to understand a little about each of these systems. Behavior, we'll get to later. We'll start here with what you really need to know about the first two items on the list, as represented by your brain (physiology) and your mind (cognition). A basic understanding of both is a prerequisite for understanding that you can control your emotions. That you can *change* them. That even when they feel all consuming, you are not, in fact, your emotions. But they do belong to you and are yours alone, and that means you can do with them what you will.

Philosophers could fill entire books about the relationship between mind and brain and the nature of thought and consciousness. In fact, many have; so if you find that you're interested in these topics, you can look for those books. But I'm warning you now that if you do, you're going to read all about dualism, materialism, and idealism, not to mention be exposed to heavy use of the word *phenomena*—and that's just for starters. For our purposes here, we just need to agree that what we're discussing when we talk about the brain is the physical structure—the roughly three-pound mass of about a hundred billion neurons protected by the skull—the organ that orchestrates the nervous system and, really, the whole body. When we talk about the *brain,* emotions are the electrical and chemical signals therein.

What we mean by the *mind* is consciousness and cognition, as well as emotion, in the sense we usually think about it—that is, the feelings that emotions give us. In general, we can define the mind largely in terms of how it functions—what it *does*. Along with thought, self-awareness, and emotion, the mind generates perception, reason, attention, judgment, will, memory, subjectivity, ideas, intention, intellect, imagination, and understanding. The mind is what we think and what we feel. When we find the balance of these last two, we're talking about not just mind, but also Wise Mind.

The skills you'll learn in this book are mostly about changing your mind: your emotions, your thoughts, your choices about how you behave. That's the stuff you can work with directly. To be effective at that work, it helps to have a little grounding in what's happening with emotion in the *brain*.

EMOTION IN THE BRAIN

To understand emotion and the experience of emotion, the most important parts of the brain to know about are the amygdala and the prefrontal cortex. The amygdala, a small almond-shaped area deep inside the brain near the brain stem, is part of the limbic system, a complex group of brain structures that support memory, behavior, motivation, and, above all else, emotion. The amygdala is responsible for initially activating an emotion. If you are looking for where Emotion Mind *is*, this is the closest you are going to get. (Fair warning: The brain, the limbic system, and the neurochemical and physiological basis of emotion are all very, very complex. I am really boiling it down here so you'll get the gist, but I'm afraid you are not going to be able to qualify for a PhD on the basis of what you read here.)

The prefrontal cortex (PFC) is located on the outside of the brain, right up in the front. Slap a hand to your forehead, and if it weren't for your skull, you might bruise your PFC. The PFC is the MVP of regulating emotion. If Logic Mind had a home, it would be here in the prefrontal cortex. It's the prefrontal cortex that allows you to reach Wise Mind.

Emotion is primarily governed by the amygdala. The amygdala is a very old, relatively primitive part of the brain—it's literally reptilian, as you'll see if you ever have a chance to do brain surgery on, say, a turtle. You'd find an amygdala in there, too (and not nearly so much of what else you'd find in the human brain). The amygdala functions as an alarm system. But since it's an alarm system originally installed for dinosaurs, it is more attuned to the concerns of iguanodons than modern humans. When something threatens, the amygdala sets off a cascade of events in the body that you know as "fight or flight": the most basic emotional response. (It's also the most basic form of stress, as one exciting part of the fight-or-flight response is the flooding of the body with stress hormones.) Fight or flight is very useful if you're about to be buried in a landslide or eaten by something much larger than you. But it is much less so if you're only facing an angry boss or a big traffic jam; in those situations, all you are left with is the oversupply of stress hormones without any practical need for them. The amygdala has no way of sorting out an ordinary kind of challenge from a life-threatening emergency, so the responses it produces are often ineffective, at best, and often make matters worse rather than better.

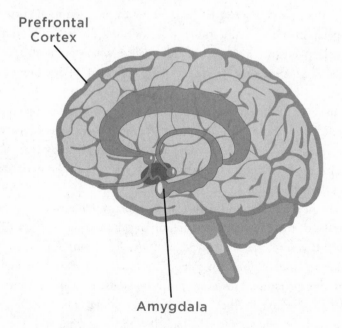

Prefrontal
Cortex

Amygdala

The amygdala's emotional range is quite narrow, running pretty much exclusively from fear to anger. It produces the jolts that get us to *act . . . now*. This is great for what all organisms need to do before they can do anything else at all: survive. To that end, the brain holds on to negatives about ten times as much as it does positives. If that's what it takes to get us to do what we must to stay alive, and therefore at least theoretically be able to reproduce, then by golly, that is what the brain is going to do. But it doesn't exactly enhance our enjoyment of life. The amygdala is excellent at alerting us to, and equipping us to address, threats to our real, physical safety. That dinosaur part of our brain is all over it when we need to escape a predator. But it is inadequate for handling disappointments, frustrations, annoyances, (nonlethal) conflict, and other modern danger zones.

As the mammalian brain evolved over time, gaining mass and complexity, the amygdala at the core remained largely unchanged. But the architecture around it grew and changed dramatically. Key among these upgrades was the addition of an extra layer on the outside, including the prefrontal cortex. The PFC is a center of higher thinking, and it functions as the brakes to the amygdala's alarm. With the prefrontal cortex, we are capable of more than automatically heeding distress calls from the amygdala. We can also interpret and analyze what's going on. We can think about the message we are receiving and what we are going to do about it.

This is the crux of the matter: the parts of the brain that start up emotion and the parts of the brain that control emotion *are different parts*. This is where our problems start, where emotions can get away from us. Wise Mind is a way of getting your brain to work as if all the parts are playing on the same team.

Imagine you are walking in nature and happen upon a snake coiled in the middle of the path (and you are among those of us who do *not* like snakes). If you rely on the amygdala alone, your course of action is clear: you either look around for something to clobber it with or hightail it back out of nature. However, if you make use of your prefrontal cortex and the "Whoa, Nellie!" it is likely providing, you have more options. You can recognize it for the harmless garter snake it is. You can remember that you're in a region where there are no poisonous snakes. You can, heh, realize you are actually in a tizzy about a stick that only *looks*—for a second, out of the corner of your eye—like a snake. Or you can hear the rattle and decide that, yes, getting out of the woods ASAP is quite a good plan, now that you think about it.

Now, imagine you're walking in nature and happen upon your teenage daughter in full eye-rolling mode. The amygdala would be eager to help you out in this situation, too. It might signal you to shout at her or get you wishing you could wipe that smirk right off her face. You are drawing on the PFC when instead you realize that she is *not* a snake after all and presents no immediate danger, despite her uncanny ability to press all your buttons. With the PFC, you can pause to consider the difficulties of her struggle to become her own person by pulling away from her parents or decide to ignore her dramatic sighs as best you can or resolve to call a friend later to commiserate about the trials of parenting.

Thanks to the amygdala, you are primed to take immediate action to secure your survival when you need to. Thanks to the prefrontal cortex, you do not *have* to send a dinosaur in to solve your less urgent, but still important, human problems. In your big human brain, you've got other apps for that.

But there's a catch. The amygdala has what amounts to high-speed broadband access, with dedicated lines running from all of your senses and to other parts of the brain. But—and you would never stand for this from your Internet provider—the information coming in isn't always very precise, thanks to how fast it is moving. The good news is that it does help you get in gear just as fast, because there's a direct connection from the amygdala to the parts of the brain that get you to *move*, bypassing all higher thinking. When the amygdala has a message to get out, it sends it out fast and loud. The whole point is to make that message very hard to ignore. Your life is on the line! You do not have time to sit around thinking about all the possible motives of the saber-toothed tiger before you or calculating the height of the cliff you are about to go over. You need to get the heck out of there! The brain is set up such that when the amygdala calls 9-1-1, it does not risk getting a busy signal—if you'll pardon the mixed metaphor.

The prefrontal cortex, meanwhile, operates more like it still has dial-up service. Its messages will get there, but delivery will take longer and may require following a more circuitous pathway. Those messages will also be more accurate as a result of their more deliberate pace. En route, they can be evaluated, compared to previous memories and experiences, or subjected to problem solving. But these pathways are shut down in the face of danger or stress, because that's the first thing the dinosaur brain does when it takes charge. And you're left without immediate access to the reasoning abilities that would allow you to filter your reactions. The alarm bell rings loud and strong, and is entirely unconcerned with whether the brakes are working.

What all this means is that emotions can hijack your thoughts much more easily and quickly than your thoughts can tame your emotions. And yet taming your emotions can be done. The hijacking part comes naturally to all of us. The taming part just takes a little more practice.

> Let's not forget that the little emotions are the great captains of our lives, and we obey them without realizing it.
>
> VINCENT VAN GOGH

THE CYCLE OF EMOTION

Thanks to the amygdala and its superfast connections, emotions can seem to happen in a flash. One second you are not experiencing any particular emotion and then WHAM! the next second you're in deep. Emotions can also build up, or reveal themselves, gradually. But no matter how short or long an emotional experience is or seems, it never just strikes like lightning, descending fully formed from the heavens for an instant and then retreating just as quickly, leaving no visible trace in the sky. Every experience of emotion actually has six distinct parts to it, though you have to slow down to see them or they can all blur together into one big, bright bolt. As with actual lightning, what seems to happen in a flash really has many components. With lightning, there's a sequence: a buildup of electrical charge in a cloud, environmental conditions that allow its release, response from objects on the ground, and a big release of light, heat, and sound. Emotion isn't always as attention-getting—though, of course, it can be—but there is always a distinct sequence: a prompting event, an interpretation of that event, a physical response, an urge to act, some action, and, finally, the aftereffects. This is the universal structure of all emotional experiences.

Understanding the various parts of the experience of emotion is actually the key to slowing down the emotional response enough so you control it, rather than it controlling you. And controlling emotions is an excellent idea, because if left unimpeded, the cycle of emotion would like nothing better than to start all over again. One of the aftereffects of an emotion can be the triggering of a whole new round. Sometimes it's another round of the same emotion, still needing to be processed; other times, it's a secondary emotion sprouting Hydra-like from the base of the first one. Or the prompting event may have created physiological changes or neurochemical changes in the brain—or the interpretation of that event did—and those changes can set off another cycle of emotion.

The Cycle of Emotion

Becoming aware of the cycle of emotion—what it is, how it affects you, and how you can interrupt it—is a way of being more mindful of emotion. In understanding the six component parts, you are practicing Wise Mind.

1. Prompting event
2. Interpretation
3. Physical response
4. Urge to act
5. Action
6. Aftereffects

There are two key things about emotions happening in a cycle. One is that a cycle can be interrupted. The other is that emotions are temporary, coming and going like waves. One may be crashing on you right now; but if you wait a moment, you may find yourself high and dry again. Once you learn to identify and tune in to the phases of an emotional response, you'll be able to choose how to best respond to an emotion, rather than be swept along by a dictatorial amygdala or habitual and unproductive reactions. *Each component of the cycle of emotions offers its own possibilities for intervention.* But you have to be able to identify the component before you can make any changes in it.

Any emotional experience begins with a *prompting event*, or *trigger*—that is, something that happens either within yourself or in your environment. Whatever actually happens, it always goes through the filter of *your interpretation*—your evaluation and understanding of what happened, your beliefs and assumptions about it, the way you explain it to yourself. Together, the event and your interpretation result in a *physical response* in your body. If you tune in, you will be able to notice the effects, such as flushed cheeks, increased heart rate, or butterflies in your stomach. Your physical response also includes facial expression and body language—a grimace, say, or clenched fists.

At the same time, you will also experience an *urge to act*. Whatever the emotion, the trigger, or the interpretation, it will bring with it a desire to do something in response. This may or may not end up being what you *do* do, but it is interesting to take note of what you want to do, or feel like doing, in those first moments. Next in the cycle of emotion comes your *action*—what you actually do—like taking to your bed or hugging someone or yelling. These are things you do on purpose (even though you may not always feel like you are really in control of them), as opposed to things that happen more automatically, like shivering or bursting into tears or tensing up. That sort of automatic thing counts as physical response. Words count as actions. So, in this category, you tally what you say right along with what you do.

The final stage of an emotional experience is *aftereffects*. This is the way the emotional experience affects you, your state of mind, your other emotions, your behavior, your thoughts, your memory, and your body.

LIVING IN WISE MIND
Burt Feels Really Mad

Here's an example of how the cycle of emotion works in real life. Keep in mind that this is just one example and that emotional experience comes in many shapes and sizes. The prompting event or physical response may be big or small, the interpretation may be almost instantaneous or thoroughly considered, the urge to act and the action may be dramatic or subtle, and the aftereffects depend on all of the above, not to mention where you started. The whole thing can be dramatic or subtle, and each stage may be obvious or difficult to identify. An emotional experience can be a onetime, finite thing, or it can be recurring. And sometimes going through a cycle of one emotion can kick off another emotion and then another whole cycle.

Burt's experience is somewhere in the middle: Late one Saturday night, Burt was up, waiting for his son Jonah to get home . . . again. Jonah's curfew was midnight and, as it had happened so often before, that time came and went with no sign of Jonah (*prompting event*). As the minutes ticked by, Burt had plenty of time to sit there and review what was happening: "Jonah is late because he is irresponsible, and he has no respect for rules or consideration of me" (*interpretation*). Burt felt it in his body too: his jaw was clenched, his breathing was shallow, and his face felt hot (*physical response*). What Burt really wanted was to give that kid a piece of his mind (*urge to act*). What Burt actually did was stay rooted in his chair, pretending to read the book in his lap and mentally rehearsing a script for just what he would say to his woefully late son (*action*). When Jonah finally walked through the door, there was enough shouting to wake the rest of the family. Burt was then left feeling exhausted, wrung out, frustrated, and determined to find a better way to handle the situation in the future (*aftereffects*). ⦿

WISE MIND REVIEW

When Burt made his way into my office, unspooling this story (among others), I gave him an exercise that I give to most of my patients—the Wise Mind Review. In my line of work, it's a common exercise—and a powerful one; don't let its simplicity fool you.

Completing a Wise Mind Review guides you in reflecting on an emotional experience so that you can identify its essential parts and, therefore, identify the options for intervening to change the experience and the outcome for you. Breaking an emotion into component parts also makes it easier to get a handle on what can often be overwhelming. If you take it no further than that, it can still provide relief. Using the full extent of the exercise, however, will allow you to successfully regulate your emotions. All it takes is getting to know your emotions a little better: what causes them, what effects they have, how you think about them, and what you do about them. Basically, you take note of each part of the cycle of the emotion you experienced.

With the Wise Mind Review, you'll figure out specifically what you are feeling—and you'll do it in writing. I don't expect you to write down everything about every emotion every time you feel one. But the more you do this review in writing, the quicker and easier it will become for you to do it in your mind, on the fly. With practice, you'll be able to do this more automatically. But at first, you'll need to spend a little time working step by step through a specific emotion that's bothering you—and doing so on paper.

Be sure to begin with an emotion that's moderately distressing and a onetime instance, not some big, horrible issue or something that's been plaguing you for a long time. Think of the last time something got you upset and work with that. It's as good a place to start as any.

Your Wise Mind Living Journal

The most informative Wise Mind book is the one you are going to write yourself. You are going to be doing a lot of exercises along the way on your journey to Wise Mind Living, and most of those exercises work best when you do them in writing. It's a way of being mindful, as well as a way of keeping track of your progress. Sometimes one "homework" assignment will require you to look back to and build on some other work you've already done. Sometimes the process of writing works to slow down or clarify your thinking or reactions. Sometimes it allows you to get to a much-needed objective stance.

That's all by way of saying: sharpen your pencils and get your hands on whatever receptacle for your words you're most comfortable with. You can dedicate a notebook or binder for this purpose or keep a blog (one you keep private) or tell your tale to dictation software, for all I care. Just take this moment to decide where you are going to do your Wise Mind work, and then set it up however you need to: fill your ink well, unroll your parchment, register a domain name, whatever.

WISE MIND LIVING PRACTICE
Wise Mind Review

This is a version of a classic CBT/DBT exercise, though there are a million similar exercises found elsewhere. It's sometimes called a Thought Record. You're going to use it to help you get into Wise Mind and to help you put Wise Mind into practice.

The eight points of the exercise are listed briefly here; more-detailed suggestions about each step follow after the basic instructions.

Choose a *recent* emotional reaction to reflect on. You are going to break it down into its component parts. In your Wise Mind Living journal, write down:

1. **The name of the emotion you're experiencing**
2. **The emotion's intensity,** on a scale from zero to ten
3. **The trigger,** or the who, what, when, and where of what happened that started this emotional experience
4. **Your interpretation** of the situation as it unfolded
5. **What was going on in your body**—What were you feeling, physically, in the moment? What physical symptoms of emotion did you have?
6. **Your action urges**—What did you feel like doing? What did you want to do?
7. **What you actually did or said** in the situation—be specific
8. **The aftereffects**

Burt's Wise Mind Review

Let's imagine that Burt, as part of his quest to find a better way to handle his son's missing curfew, jotted down a partial Wise Mind Review for his late-night experience of waiting for Jonah. It might look like this:

1. Anger.
2. 7
3. Jonah missed curfew *again*.
4. Jonah does not listen to me or follow my rules because he is irresponsible and inconsiderate. I set this curfew to keep him safe, and he completely disregards me. He completely ignores the idea that something horrible could happen to him. I just can't keep doing this over and over with him.
5. Clenching jaw, breathing shallow, face hot, hands cold.
6. I really need to find some way to handle this better. I'm going to give him a piece of my mind when he gets home.

Naming the Emotion

Naming the emotion is often the trickiest part of the whole Wise Mind Review exercise. Since how you label it can affect how you express it, you need to name the emotion with care. Allow yourself to consider the question a bit. Don't assume you always know the answer right off the bat. If you label or express the "wrong" emotion—maybe a secondary feeling rather than what is actually the primary source of your upset—you may stay mired in the whole mess for longer. So pay attention to precisely what you are feeling, as best you can. (You are going to get better at this as you learn the Wise Mind Living strategies.) Make sure you think through whether you are really angry, to take one example. Or would it be more accurate to say you were embarrassed, jealous, or hurt?

When you pause to consider it, you may find that the right word to describe your emotion is not top of mind. If you'd like some suggestions to inspire your selection, you may find "The Big Eight: Families of Emotions" (page 54) helpful.

If you're still stumped about what to name your emotion, another option is to not name it at all. If you are not sure exactly what to call what you are feeling, skip this first step for now. You can come back and fill it in later, as working through the other items will sometimes clarify what should go in the first slot. Or go ahead and name it right off, picking a name that seems reasonable enough, and then come back to review your choice after you've completed the rest of the steps. If it no longer seems to be the right fit, change it!

Intensity: Zero to Ten

Don't get too caught up in exactly how you assign point values. What you call six, I might call eight, and that's perfectly okay. It's all about how you are experiencing the emotion, and all that matters is that the ranking is consistent for you: what's a six today is a six tomorrow.

One of the main reasons for noting the intensity of what you're feeling is to allow you to track change over time. You can rate how you're feeling again after you've taken some time to think the whole thing through. Has the intensity decreased at least a little bit? Are you amping yourself up further? As you practice Wise Mind Living, you can look back to see if a fight like the one you just had with your partner has always felt like a six to you or if you used to experience it as having greater or lesser intensity.

Another handy way to use this rating is to officially notice when the intensity is very high. In those cases, you may need or want to do something to calm your brain and body a bit before you proceed with anything else. If you skip that step when intensity is high, you will not be able to do your best thinking or problem solving.

Trigger and Interpretation

As important as noting what happened to set off your emotion ("What happened that prompted this reaction? What was it, within or around me, that started this emotion?") is noting your *interpretation* of what happened. If you are not careful, the trigger and the interpretation can seem like the same thing. Burt would be off target if he wrote, "Jonah's trying to piss me off" (*interpretation*) at step three, as opposed to "Jonah missed curfew" (*trigger*). The trigger is the who, what, when, and where, while the interpretation is your view of *why* and how. As in, how did this emotional reaction happen? It's a question of what caused the emotional reaction; it's not the incident that started the ball rolling, but the thoughts about that trigger that built up the emotion. Your interpretation includes your beliefs and assumptions about, and appraisals of, the prompting event—and those same things need to be kept *out* of your statement of what happened.

The next chapter contains lists of the most common types of prompting events (page 62) and interpretations (page 64)—they both tend to cluster into certain themes—that you can refer to if you need help figuring out what's setting you off or how you're thinking about it. But as a Wise Mind beginner, using a Wise Mind Review will work just fine if you simply make your best guess for now.

Physical Response

You can answer the question about what you were feeling in your body while you had an emotion by recalling your memory of the experience. But it may also be useful to look over "Signals of Emotion" (page 60) and ask yourself whether any of those examples apply. You may not always be aware of what happens to you physiologically, or you might not always think to connect a given physical feeling to having an emotion. Simply recalling as best you can is a fine way to start.

Action Urges and Actions

A surge of emotion will make you feel like taking certain actions—yelling at someone, taking to your bed, getting some fresh air, ignoring the problem, punching a wall. Then there is a separate list of the actions you actually *do* take. To whatever degree these two overlap, you should note both in their respective spots during your Wise Mind Review. Here again, your best recollection is fine; but if you want to spur your thinking a bit, you can consult the "Urge to Act and Actions" list (page 66).

Aftereffects

Aftereffects are the types of impacts the distressing situation has had on you; they are the consequences of what happened and how you responded to it. As the cycle of emotion comes toward its end—and, in the nature of cycles, back to where it started—you will experience aftereffects. What those aftereffects are, whether you identify them for what they are, and how you manage them have everything to do with whether you charge ahead into another full-blown cycle of distressing emotion or whether you have done what you need to do in order to finish that particular chapter. The "Aftereffects" list (page 68) may help you identify aftereffects that you experience.

A VERY GOOD PLACE TO START

You can use a Wise Mind Review as the first phase of a longer exercise called Wise Mind Debate (page 104). But for now it stands on its own as a sort of "getting to know you" process for you and your emotions. When you've finished writing down your responses, one through eight, reread them with an eye toward picking out where in the cycle you might want to make changes. Most commonly, the place to start is with your interpretation, and that's what the Wise Mind Debate is more specifically about. Still, you may have enough to go on here to begin evaluating whether your interpretation is in fact the correct one, the only one that fits the situation. The essential questions are: "Is there another way to look at it? And if so, might taking that stance change the rest of my emotional experience?"

If you are having an intense physical response to an emotion, that might be a better place for you to start seeking change. If being upset has given you a pounding headache, for example, your best bet may be to find a way to soothe the pain before you turn your attention to other parts of the cycle of emotion. In fact, if you are having any more than a passing physical reaction, it might make sense to start with the physiological aspect. You aren't going to have complete access to your higher-order thinking anyway if you are mired in a lizard-like visceral response. If you deactivate the alarm first, you'll be much better able to use the other parts of your brain to think about and make good choices.

Your urge to act may be where you must start if the urge threatens to become action and that action involves something like hitting someone. If your urge is to bite your fingernails or some such, curbing it may not be so urgent. If your urge is to take a walk, it might even be the solution you're looking for. But if your urge to act could hurt you or others, you should probably move changing that aspect of the emotion cycle to the top of your to-do list.

You'll find ways to accomplish all these things, and more, throughout this book. Doing a Wise Mind Review is a great prelude to all of them. Wise Mind Review by itself *is* an intervention, even before you implement any of the upcoming strategies. Just doing the exercise is likely to calm the alarm in your brain, and that's at least half the battle. Another important thing about the Wise Mind Review is that it creates a little distance between you and your emotions. It helps put you in what mindfulness experts like to promote as "observer's stance." Distance also does much to reduce the hold that emotions have on you. Paying attention to what you are feeling helps you feel less of it, and sometimes that's enough.

4

NAME THAT EMOTION

(Hint: It's One of the Big Eight)

I t was a case of emotional mistaken identity that tripped up Burt in his late-night interactions with his son. As Burt waited into the wee hours of the morning for Jonah to come home—way past curfew, again—Burt knew he was angry, angry, *angry*. Working through the experience afterward, however, he got no further than the second step of writing a Wise Mind Review before he was inspired to think differently about his conflict with Jonah. As he looked at his notes, he suddenly recognized his thoughts were about *fear* rather than *anger*. As he remembered that night, he recalled that the longer past midnight it got, the more terrible thoughts he had about what could be keeping his son: a car accident, drunkenness, a fistfight. You name it, and Burt's brain could conjure dire images of it. Looking at all that on the page, he could see it: he wasn't so much furious at his son as he was *worried* for him.

That distinction made all the difference for Burt (and Jonah). Changing the way he labeled his emotion changed what Burt thought and did, so it also changed the results he got. Burt became mindful of his emotions by using a Wise Mind Review to observe and better understand not only his emotions but also their component parts. Then he was able to work with his emotions, changing what he didn't like, accepting what he couldn't change, and reducing his suffering all the while. An important first step for Burt, or anyone, was identifying the right label for what he was feeling.

Burt experienced for himself a central tenet of Wise Mind Living: accurately identifying the emotion you are experiencing is absolutely essential to mastering that emotion. You simply must know exactly what feeling you're dealing with if you want to be able to cope with it. Or change it. Or revel in it, for that matter. Perhaps the importance of this mission explains why humans have a long, long list of words to label emotions. We can use these words to convey the finest shades of meaning, should we be so inclined. (You will find a long list of words commonly used to describe emotions on page 56.)

Yet it can be difficult to accurately label an emotion, especially in the heat of the moment, when a laundry list of options is more daunting than helpful. So here's the good news: from a purely practical perspective, you can get the job done with just eight choices. All emotions can basically be divided into eight core categories: fear, anger, sadness, shame, jealousy, and disgust on the down side, plus love and happiness to lighten things up. This limited list makes figuring out which emotion you are experiencing a more manageable task. These core categories of emotions are our "Big Eight," and each covers a lot of territory. Feeling irritated, frustrated, or enraged? File under anger. Amused, cheerful, joyful? That's happiness, happiness, and happiness you're experiencing. (Theorists love to debate exactly how many core emotions there are and what the best label for each category is. So you'll find other ways of doing this out there. But this is the version that's held up, practically speaking, with my patients.)

The Big Eight: Families of Emotions

When you take time to consider what label to place on your emotion, you are practicing mindfulness of emotion; you are clearing a path for yourself so you can then manage that emotion.

- Love
- Happiness
- Fear
- Anger
- Sadness
- Shame
- Jealousy
- Disgust

EMOTION FAMILIES

None of the Big Eight is a single, well-defined feeling; each is more like a family of related feelings. Some members of the emotion family are like twins, while others are more like second cousins—but all are clearly connected by certain shared characteristics. These characteristics may show up more forcefully in some members and more subtly in others, like the way your Uncle Mike has all that crazy carrot-top hair, but you can't see your red highlights until you are standing in the sun.

In emotion families, as in human families, variations in the group reflect differences inherent in the individual emotion, as well as differences in the circumstances under which the individual emotion comes up. Compassion and passion are quite different feelings, but they are both in the love family, and the same person or situation might bring out both in you. But circumstances can make a difference. The fear family members of jumpiness, worry, and panic, for example, are likely to arise in quite different situations, like being alone in an unfamiliar house at night, getting a bill when your bank account is low, or witnessing a serious car accident. And the wrong variation in a given circumstance is where you can run into problems with emotions—panicking about an overdue bill is not going to help anything, nor is worrying about the best thing to do when you come upon an accident. In Wise Mind, there *is* something to be learned, however, in recognizing that all of these situations bring up some form of fear. (Not everyone reacts to the same situation in the same way, of course, so you might be unfazed by a dark room, while your child is upset in one, or you might be shaken by the scene of an accident, while an off-duty EMT might calmly spring into action.)

The more you understand about these families of emotions and their distinguishing characteristics, the better you'll be able to identify and manage the emotions that happen to you. We will break down each component of an emotional experience to help you understand your emotions and how they work, so that you'll be ready and able to accept and change them. Each emotion family has a unique set of features: when and why it happens; what it looks, sounds, and feels like when you experience any variation on the theme; what you are likely to do about it; and what it feels like in the aftermath. When you are having an emotion and you go looking, you can expect to find these characteristics. And if you recognize the effects an unnamed emotion is having on you, the pattern can help you pinpoint exactly which emotion has you in its grip. In the midst of an emotional experience, it can be surprisingly difficult to correctly identify whether you are angry, afraid, sad, or what, but that is exactly what you must do to manage emotion well, no matter what the emotion may be. And when you observe your emotions with Wise Mind, you can do just that!

THE LIST

We humans have many more words to label emotions than we have core emotions, as the long lists that follow can only begin to demonstrate. Although no such list could be truly complete, I've tried to give you the most common labels to get you started in pinpointing what you're feeling.

Most Common Labels of Emotions

EMOTION	I FEEL . . .
Fear	agitated, alarmed, anxious, apprehensive, concerned, desperate, dismayed, dread, fearful, frightened, horror, hysterical, jumpy, nervous, panicked, scared, shocked, shy, tense, terror, timid, uncertain, uneasy, worried
Anger	aggravated, agitated, annoyed, antagonized, bitter, contemptuous (other than for self), contentious, contrary, cranky, cruel, destructive, displeased, enraged, exasperated, explosive, frustrated, furious, hateful, hostile, indignant, insulted, irate, irritable, irritated, mad, mean, outraged, resentful, scornful, spiteful, vengeful
Sadness	alienated, anguished, bereft, blue, bored, crushed, defeated, dejected, depressed, despairing, despondent, disappointed, discouraged, disheartened, dismayed, dispirited, displeased, distraught, down, downhearted, dreary, forlorn, gloomy, grief-stricken, hopeless, hurt, insecure, isolated, lonely, melancholy, miserable, mopey, morbid, morose, mournful, neglected, oppressed, pessimistic, pitiful, rejected, somber, sorrowful, tragic, unhappy

Shame	besmirched, chagrined, contemptuous (of self), contrite, culpable, debased, degraded, disapproving, disdainful, disgraced, disgusted (at self), dishonored, disreputable, embarrassed, guilty, hateful, humbled, humiliated, improper, infamous, invalidated, mortified, regretful, remorseful, repentant, reproachful, rueful, scandalized, scornful, sinful, stigmatized
Jealousy	competitive, covetous, deprived, distrustful, envious, greedy, grudging, jealous, overprotective, petty, possessive, resentful, rivalrous
Disgust	appalled, dislike, grossed out, insulted, intolerant, nauseated, offended, put off, repelled, repulsed, revolted, revulsion, shocked, sickened, turned off
Happiness	agreeable, amused, blissful, bubbly, cheerful, content, delighted, eager, ease, elated, enjoyment, enthusiastic, euphoric, excited, exhilarated, glad, gleeful, glowing, gratified, harmonious, hopeful, interested, jolly, joyful, jubilant, lighthearted, meaningful, merry, optimistic, peaceful, pleasure, pride, proud, relieved, relish, satisfied, thrilled, triumphant, up, well-being, zealous
Love	acceptance, admiration, adoring, affectionate, allegiance, attachment, attraction, belonging, caring, compassionate, connected, dependent, desire, devoted, faithful, friendship, interested, kind, liking, passionate, protective, respect, sympathetic, tender, vulnerable, warm

WISE MIND LIVING PRACTICE
Name That Emotion Family

This is a deceptively simple assignment: practice "catching" yourself in an emotion and then give that emotion a name. Sometimes just labeling it can be enough to defang it.

So which of the Big Eight are you experiencing? If you are able to identify the family to which your emotion belongs, you can use the long list of emotion words ("Most Common Labels of Emotions," page 56) to get more specific about your emotion. Or, if it turns out to be easier for you to move from narrower to wider, find the specific emotion you've identified on the chart to discover what family it belongs to.

You will get more adept at this as you learn more about living in Wise Mind. For now, however, it's worthwhile to do it in this most basic way. As Burt discovered, just finding the right name for what you are feeling can be enough to make a world of difference.

"I'm So Emotional"

Another category of emotion words to watch out for includes the words that simply signify that you are in an emotional state, without giving a good indication of *which* emotional state it might be. These words apply across emotion families; so if this is what you sound like as you are evaluating your emotion, try to be more specific. (If the bottom two adjectives on the following list seem odd to you, consider that even though "fine" and "okay" seem to indicate positive emotion [or lack of big emotion], they are often used as a way of denying or papering over distressing feelings.)

I feel . . .

Upset	Distressed
Stressed	Numb
Overwhelmed	Moody
Fine	Okay

LIVING IN WISE MIND
Serena Was Stuck

Serena came to me fearing she was depressed. She wasn't moving forward in her life, she told me; somehow she didn't feel motivated to do what she needed to do. Both day-to-day "to do" items and bigger-picture things were falling by the wayside too often. She felt stuck. She *was* stuck (though I didn't think she met the criteria for clinical depression). Then a dream changed her life.

It was actually a dream she'd had many times. In it, she'd step on the subway to go to work, the doors would whoosh shut behind her, and the train would take off full speed and take her wherever *it* wanted to go. It was more like a roller-coaster ride than a commute, with Serena chucked out at seemingly random destinations.

It was a scary dream. Serena knew what the classic interpretation would be: this was an anxiety dream, showing she felt out of control of her own life. Yet she told me that she didn't feel particularly anxious. I suggested an exercise to clarify the emotions in the dream to help her understand what she was feeling—what message she might be sending herself while asleep. I asked her to retell the dream as if it were happening in real time and to give speaking parts to all the major players in the dream. In this case, that would include the train, since it was clearly a star of the show, despite being an inanimate object.

And so Serena began the story again: "So, I'm walking into the station like I do every morning . . ." She took me through it moment by moment. When she described the train zooming off for some unknown, unrequested destination, I asked what the train would say at that moment if she asked where it was going or what it was doing. She answered right away: "You think you are so important, you think *I* should do what you want. Big shot, huh? Think the world revolves around you? You're such a loser."

Serena suddenly realized that the train was parroting the things her sister would say to her. And Serena had lodged her sister's berating in her own head, coming to see herself this way and feeling worthless. This was an "ah-ha!" moment for Serena, revealing to her a big obstacle that she hadn't been able to see: what she was feeling was not, in fact, anxiety, or even anger at her sister, but shame. Once she identified her core emotion and understood more about how her chronic experience of shame was affecting her, Serena could challenge the feeling when it came up in her life. Being able to do that turned out to be the key to getting unstuck. Serena now knew she deserved better for—and from!—herself, so she found she was able to go get it. As she became gentler with herself, she began moving forward, and as she moved forward, she felt less self-critical. ◍

Poor Faulkner. Does he really think big emotions come from big words? He thinks I don't know the ten-dollar words. I know them all right. But there are older and simpler and better words, and those are the ones I use.

ERNEST HEMINGWAY

THE CYCLE OF EMOTION IN THE BIG EIGHT

The cycle of emotion has the same component parts no matter which of the Big Eight you're dealing with. But each family of emotion has its own hallmark pattern of common triggers, interpretations, and actions (both what you do and what you feel like doing). Each part of the cycle offers a chance to intervene with a distressing emotion, but only if you are mindful of what each component is all about.

Signals of Emotion

The most common physical symptoms of emotion are pretty much the same for all emotion families.

- Breathing fast or breathlessness
- Clenching hands or making fists
- Clenching teeth or jaw
- Crying
- Diarrhea or vomiting
- Difficulty swallowing or lump in the throat
- Dizziness
- Dry mouth
- Fast heartbeat
- Fatigue, tiredness, or low energy (despite enough sleep)
- Flushed, red, or hot face
- Getting cold
- Headache
- Jitters

- Loss of appetite (nothing tastes good) or ravenous hunger
- Pain or hollowness in the chest or gut
- Shaking
- Slumped posture
- Stomachache, cramps, feeling of heaviness in the stomach
- Suffocating or choking sensation
- Sweating
- Tight or tense muscles

Prompting Events

Your first focus should be on the situation part of the equation. In the cycle of emotion, this is the prompting event (the trigger). The Big Eight are designed to be triggered in specific kinds of situations, and they are only useful in those situations; the wrong emotion for the situation is a recipe for trouble. It is possible to feel fear in a situation that simply isn't scary or isn't really dangerous (we'll get into the problems with and solutions to that in later chapters). Often what happens, though, is that you *think* you are having one emotion, but really you are having a different one. One way to straighten this out is to correctly identify the emotion by correctly identifying the prompting event or situation.

If you are stuck on naming the emotion ("Hmmm, I'm pretty sure I'm mad! But what else could it be?"), then thinking a bit about what brought it on can help clarify. ("Okay, so no one said word one to me about the fact that I brought that project in ahead of deadline.") If you can generalize about what prompted it ("It's like no one thought my work was worth anything") to match it to one of the items on the "Most Common Types of Prompting Events" list ("not feeling valued"), then you may realize that you are really more sad than angry. Herein lies another benefit of doing a Wise Mind Review in writing: your choice of words can tell you a lot about what you are feeling. Of course, you use words when you do this in your head, but you can't reflect on them as you can when those words are committed to the page.

Most Common Types of Prompting Events

EMOTION	PROMPTING EVENTS
Fear	Danger or perception of danger
	Unfamiliar situation
	Darkness
	Being alone
	Belief that something bad is going to happen to you
	Situation similar to one in which you have been hurt or seen others hurt in the past
	Anticipating criticism, disapproval, or rejection
	Expecting failure
Anger	Losing power or status
	Being insulted
	Pain (physical or emotional) or the threat of pain
	Someone taking something from you (or the belief that someone has)
	Something not turning out as you expected
	Disruption of an important activity
	Not getting something you want
	Having to stop doing something you are enjoying
Sadness	Loss of something important to you
	Losing someone important to you
	Thinking about loss or separation
	Rejection
	Not having what you want
	Not having what you think you need
	Getting what you don't want
	Something turning out badly
	Not feeling valued
	Being disapproved of or disliked
	Being powerless
	The company of someone in pain (physical or emotional)
	Thinking about others' troubles
Jealousy	Someone else has something you want or need
	You earned or are entitled to something you don't have—but someone else does have
	Important relationship is in jeopardy
	Someone taking away things that are important to you (or threatening to)

Shame	Doing something you believe is wrong
	Others discovering you did something wrong
	Thinking of something you did wrong in the past
	Something private being exposed
	Being made fun of
	Being publicly criticized
	Having your integrity attacked
	Being betrayed
	Failure (especially in something you consider yourself good at)
	Rejection
	Getting criticism when you expected praise
	Having your emotions invalidated
Disgust	Interacting with something that could make you ill or that could otherwise hurt you
	Interacting with someone whose words or actions could hurt you or your reputation
	Interacting with someone you really dislike
Happiness	Success at a particular task
	Getting what you want
	Getting something you worked hard for or worried about
	Being respected
	Receiving praise
	Something turning out as you hoped
	Having your expectations exceeded
	A fun surprise
	Acceptance
	Belonging
	Being loved
	Being liked
	Receiving affection
	Being with people you love
	Being with people you like
	Physical pleasure
Love	Spending a lot of time with someone
	Sharing a special experience with someone
	Someone gives you something you want or need
	Someone does what you want or need them to do
	Communicating really well with someone
	Physical closeness or sex

Adapted from Marsha Linehan's *Skills Training Manual for Treating Borderline Personality Disorder*

Interpretations

Your thoughts and interpretations of a prompting event play a huge role in your experience of emotion. Wise Mind helps you make sure your thoughts are on target and shows you how to clean them up when they are problematic; in fact, chapter 7 is all about that. For now, you can use the themes listed here to help you identify your exact emotion. Later, you'll work more with reality-testing your interpretations; to do that, familiarity with these patterns will come in handy.

Common Interpretations

EMOTION	INTERPRETATIONS
Fear	This is dangerous.
	I really need help.
	I'm not going to get what I need.
	This is a going to be a big failure.
	I am going to lose this relationship.
	I'm not going to be able to handle this.
	This is out of control.
	I can't help it.
	I can't do this.
	I used to be really good at this.
	This is going to hurt me.
	I am going to die.
Anger	She's trying to hurt me.
	He's blocking my goal.
	This is unfair.
	This is not the way it is supposed to be.
	I am right, and that is all there is to it.
	This is just wrong.
Sadness	This hurts.
	This is hopeless.
	I'll never get what I want.
	I'll never get what I need.
	I'm really going to miss him/her/this.

Shame	I hate my body (thighs, hair, belly, nose, . . .). I am worthless. I am better than this. I let them down. I am so stupid. It's dumb to feel this way. I'm not good enough. Why can't I be more like her? I'm such a loser. Who's ever going to love me?
Jealousy	I am missing out. They're going to take what I have. I should have that, too.
Disgust	I don't like this at all. That is so gross. Get that away from me. I can't stomach this. You make me sick. I hate this.
Happiness	This is so nice. I feel great. Things are going great. This pleases me.
Love	He loves me. She needs me. He appreciates me. She is so pretty. He has a great personality. I can always count on her. He is perfect.

Adapted from Marsha Linehan's *Skills Training Manual for Treating Borderline Personality Disorder*

Urge to Act and Actions

When Burt correctly relabeled his late-night feelings toward his son—recognizing the fear he felt—he found that his anger was almost instantly nonexistent. Something else big changed at the same time—the action he felt like taking. It wasn't long before Jonah once again asked to borrow the car for the evening, and instead of lecturing or threatening dire consequences for lateness or employing the *Do you not remember how late you got home last time?* death stare, Burt's gut reaction was different. He saw a new angle from which to approach the topic. And when Burt communicated fear rather than fury, he got a very different response from his son.

Jonah wasn't suddenly on time for every curfew, of course, but he did begin to text his dad about his whereabouts when he wasn't home on time. Burt still didn't like the lateness, but as long as knew his son was okay, he no longer spent his weekend nights fuming until all hours. When Burt named his emotion properly, it changed both his action urge and his actions. That changed the outcome in practical terms *and* reduced the amount of suffering his emotional response put him through.

All this is by way of saying: pay attention to what you feel compelled to do as an emotion overtakes you, as well as what you actually do. Doing so can help you identify the emotion, if that is what you need. It can also point the way to constructive responses rather than destructive reactions. Your choice of action has a lot to do with how quickly an emotion subsides. You will learn a lot more about how to control this part of the emotion cycle in chapter 8. But you won't need to learn all the details to benefit from identifying your urge to act, your actions, and their similarities and differences.

Urge to Act and Actions

EMOTION	*I felt like I wanted to . . .* OR *What I did was . . .*
Fear	cry, whimper, scream/yell, call for help, hide, leave, move quickly, avoid, stare, talk too much, run away, stop talking, freeze, speak nervously or quickly
Anger	attack verbally, criticize, attack physically, curse, yell/scream/shout, complain, gesture aggressively, stomp, brood, withdraw, clench fists/muscles, hit something, throw or break something, blow up, slam doors, grit teeth, walk out

Sadness	withdraw, not try or not bother, be passive, be inactive, slump, keep my eyes closed, quit, cry, be alone, sleep, mope, give up, cancel plans
Shame	withdraw, cover my face, hide, grovel, lower my eyes/look down or away, avoid the people who knew I'd done wrong, slump, apologize, ask for forgiveness, give a gift, make amends, repair damage
Jealousy	try to control others, hoard things for myself, poke my nose into other people's business, avoid, deny others' merit, be close-minded, close my eyes, review all I lack, compare what I have with what someone else has, criticize someone else, threaten the other person, make accusations of disloyalty, spy on the other person, cling or be needy, do something to get even
Disgust	move away, be mean, criticize, grimace, clench muscles, make a face, throw away, cover up, clean up
Happiness	smile, laugh, express positive feelings, hug someone, say positive things, be talkative, jump up and down
Love	say "I love you," make eye contact, physical affection, smile, express positive feelings to someone, do something another person wants or needs, share an experience, spend time with someone, hug, take care of, share, love

Adapted from Marsha Linehan's *Skills Training Manual for Treating Borderline Personality Disorder*

Aftereffects

The final component of the cycle of emotion is a tricky one, no matter what the emotion. If you are not mindful of the aftereffects of emotion, you may end up kicking off a whole new round of distress rather than finding one last exit ramp.

Part of what Burt had to sort out in order to manage his emotions was a particular kind of aftereffect: a secondary emotion. A secondary emotion is an emotion we develop in the wake of a primary emotion, though sometimes it can be hard to sort them out in a chicken/egg kind of way. Which came first? Burt stumbled in answering that, but he got better results once he figured out that fear was the real core of what he was feeling, and his anger—because he was indeed feeling angry—was a secondary emotion. In other words, his anger was an aftereffect. It is always more effective to address the primary emotion rather than the secondary one, at least to begin with.

Common Aftereffects

EMOTION	AFTEREFFECTS
Fear	Loss of focus
	Loss of control
	Memories of other frightening situations or events
	Thoughts of what else could go wrong
	Numbness or shock
	Anger or shame
Anger	Thinking about what made you angry, over and over
	Thinking about or dealing with *only* what made you angry
	Thinking of another time something made you angry
	Imagining things that will make you angry in the future
	Paying attention only to anger and other negative emotions
	Numbness
	Shame or fear
Sadness	Thinking about what made you sad, over and over
	Thinking of other things that make you sad
	Blaming or criticizing yourself or someone else
	Inability to think of positive things
	Numbness or shock
	Anger, shame, or fear
Shame	Shutting down
	Impulsive behavior
	Seeking distraction
	Avoiding thinking about what you did
	Believing you are defective
	Resolving to change
	Numbness
	Alienation
	Anger, sadness, or fear

Jealousy	Withdrawing
	Becoming hypervigilant
	Thinking over and over about what you don't have or what others have that you want
	Fear or shame
Disgust	Thinking over and over about the thing you dislike
	Becoming hypersensitive
	Fear or shame
Happiness	Friendliness
	Politeness
	Optimism
	Memories of other happy times
	Anticipation of future happiness
	Doing something nice for someone else
	Resistance to getting annoyed or worried
Love	Thinking someone is perfect
	Forgetfulness
	Being distracted
	Daydreaming
	Openness and trust
	Memories of other people you've loved or been loved by
	Memories of other times, things, or situations you have loved
	Thoughts of other positive events
	Self-confidence

Adapted from Marsha Linehan's *Skills Training Manual for Treating Borderline Personality Disorder*

EMOTION VERSUS MOOD

Emotions occur in distinct episodes that rise and fall quickly, if we let them. The trouble is, we often don't let them. They may rise up all of a sudden all right, but we have a tendency to make them stick around rather than let them recede as they naturally would. When they stick around longer, they become moods, which is excellent when the emotion is happiness and we wind up announcing to whoever will listen, "I am in *such* a good mood!" Less awesome is when we prolong a distressing emotion to the point that we are in the kind of mood that, if we were cartoons, would be signified by dark clouds hovering over our heads.

Once an emotion has been triggered by something outside ourselves—a thoughtless comment from a colleague, say—every thought we have about it is an opportunity to internally retrigger the emotion, which is just what will happen if our thoughts run along the lines of "She is really mean" or "I hate feeling this way." Every action has a chance at retriggering us, too. (In this example, if you were to march into your colleague's office to give her a piece of your mind, you would pretty much be guaranteed to keep feeling angry for the duration of the argument, at least.) Other times, retriggering follows an external event that is recurring, such as sadness over missing someone who is gone for good.

When we keep retriggering and retriggering an emotion—or when life does it for us—an emotion can turn into a mood. If moods hang around long enough, they can verge over into the territory of diagnosable emotional problems, such as depression or an anxiety disorder. If they stick around an incredibly long time, they can become so habitual that they actually become emotional traits or parts of our personalities—a part of who we *are*. Imagine someone who feels so gray for so long that everyone just thinks of him as Joe the Pessimist. Some more complicated moods, like grief and romantic and parental love, follow a bit of a different pattern. But, in general, the difference between an emotion and a mood is how long it lasts. Emotions are meant to be short; to the degree that we can keep the distressing ones that way, we can avoid moods we really don't want to be stuck in. (It also means that if we want to hang onto positive emotions, we have to work at it a bit because they, too, will fade as quickly as they come unless we use our thoughts and actions to hang onto the good feelings.)

Whether an emotion sloughs off or sticks around is largely within your control. Wise Mind skills help you lengthen the good and hasten the bad. When you reach advanced levels, these skills can help with moods and even emotional disorders, though they are designed more specifically for managing everyday, moment-to-moment emotional challenges—so you'll do best to start there. With practice, you'll be able to let the distressing emotions go, as they are meant to, before they settle in and become bad moods. Or worse.

UNDERSTANDING EMOTIONS

The cycle of emotion explains how emotional experiences unfold and, therefore, when and how you can intervene to *change* the nature of the experience—that is, decrease or eliminate what's distressing you. That's only one piece of the puzzle of understanding emotions, though. The next chapter lines up another important one: What's the point of emotions anyway? If they can be so painful, why do I have them? Why would I want them? (But you should want them!) What good are they? Getting a grip on the answers goes a long way toward your being able to *accept* your emotions. The combination of change and acceptance is the very heart of Wise Mind Living.

5

WHAT GOOD
ARE MY EMOTIONS?

The Good in the Bad
and the Bad in the Good

Naming your emotions sets you off on the journey to managing them, but you're not going to get far down the road without also *understanding* them—or, more exactly, understanding what your emotions do for you. Without that key insight, your first idea about how to "manage" a troublesome emotion might well be to get rid of it all together—or to wish you could, anyway. That's not helpful, not only because it is impossible (your emotions are hardwired and here to stay) and counterproductive (avoidance or denial of problematic emotions will compound the negative effects of those emotions), but also because your emotions demand attention for the very good reason that they are useful.

Actually, they are not just useful; they are also crucial to our very survival as a species. There's evolutionary pressure to keep fear, anger, and other "negative" emotions as part of our repertoire—as well as happiness and love. Our ancient ancestors' emotional responses were part of what defined who was "fittest" and, therefore, who survived. Emotions literally help humans to stay alive in the moment—that is, fear helps us escape from danger; love makes us want to protect others. They also help over the long term in the evolutionary sense—reproducing and passing down our genes from generation to generation (fear leads us to live in social groups for protection, and love makes us want to have sex).

The way emotions come on so rapidly is central to the survival advantage they offer. The whole idea is to get us on the stick, and quick, when important events happen. If emotions took their own sweet time to build up within us, then whatever they were trying to alert us to or prepare us for could be over and done with before we felt anything. The same pressures have also ensured that emotions drain away as quickly as they "light up"—at least they are supposed to, because it behooves us to not continue having all our automatic responses to an emotion indefinitely. Among other reasons that this isn't desirable is that we want to be able to notice when the emotion is triggered again. The rapid rise and fall is simply what emotions do, thanks to millions of years of experience. We can make them stick around, and we often do, but usually that only leads to trouble.

Our brain's amygdala—the seat of fear and anger—is testament to the evolutionary advantages of those emotions, despite the trouble they cause. We can trace the amygdala back to the brains of the earliest humanlike creatures, further back through to the earliest primates, through early mammals, and all the way into the reptiles. The forces of evolution kept that structure of the brain around, even as the complexity of the brain expanded and increased. This has only happened because the amygdala provides an edge to those who have it over those who don't. The benefits we receive from emotions today may be less about life or death than those measured in evolutionary time, but they are just as real, as are—maybe even especially—the benefits we get from the so-called negative emotions (fear, anger, shame, sadness).

I should say, however, that there really is no such thing as a "negative" emotion. It's hard to hang that handle on emotions when they serve us so well—or at least they do when we manage them effectively. Emotions themselves are not good or bad; rather, the problems we have with emotions come from the distress—and stress—they sometimes cause us. When I want to sound all therapist-y, I refer to them as "distressing" emotions, though even the emotions that distress us serve an important purpose in our lives.

When they are not keeping us *alive*, emotions lend a hand in other ways. They get us ready to act, preparing us to do what we need to do. They help us solve problems. Emotions and the expressions that come with them can help us communicate with others—and with *ourselves*. Emotions can motivate us to act and can help us prioritize and organize what we're going to do. They provide a shortcut when we do not have time to thoroughly think through what we are going to do or say. They can help us influence others and tune us in to what others are feeling. Emotions clue us in to and help us cope with threats, as well as help us identify and respond to opportunities. We need to know what is happening in our world, and emotions are often the way we find out.

The truth is, we'd all be lost without our emotions. We experience and use emotions every single day.

When we are living in Wise Mind, we take what we can from emotions, honoring both their immediate benefits and their advantages on an evolutionary scale. In Wise Mind, we seek to hear the messages that emotions have for us and heed their lessons. But this is not to say we celebrate suffering ("I am so glad to be suffering with all this sadness! Think how much I am learning from this!") and let it go at that. Rather, in Wise Mind, we appreciate what emotions offer while also aiming to (1) tone down excess intensity and unwanted effects as much as possible and (2) learn to handle, with grace, what we can't eliminate. It's the same old Wise Mind song: acceptance and change, change and acceptance.

FEAR

Fear is the most obvious example of an emotion, even a painful one, contributing to human survival. Fear hardwires into us the urge to run or hide from whatever threatens our safety or sends us in to battle that threat as prepared as we can be. And it's not just because of our feelings; the physiological changes we experience with this emotion are quite specifically tailored to either of those ways of coping with a threat—fight or flight. For example, when something frightens us, our bodies release a jolt of epinephrine, which prevents fatigue and allows us to run or to fight beyond our normal endurance. Nonvital bodily systems slow or shut down so that all energy can be spent on the battle (or flight) at hand. Digestion essentially stops, because in truly dangerous circumstances, it would be a waste of energy. When we are in a state of fear, our blood actually clots more efficiently—which would come in handy if we were wounded in the face of danger. The mind becomes narrowly focused on getting past the danger; we think of pretty much nothing else. Even the sounds we make when we are scared, though they may feel automatic, serve to let anyone friendly know we need help and to warn others of danger. These are very valuable responses to have, and our very ancestors are the humans who had them in the greatest supply and thus survived to have offspring who survived, who also had offspring, and so on, right down to us.

In the context of your life today, most of the times that you feel fear are not actually life-or-death situations. You probably aren't going to require super-duper clotting as you worry about being able to pay the bills. But the increase in focus may still prove convenient. And experiencing the emotion flags your low bank balance as an issue that needs to be attended to. What would happen if lack of funds *didn't* concern you, so you paid it no mind and never changed your approach to earning or spending? Generally speaking, fear functions as an alarm bell that something needs to be dealt with—*now*.

SHAME

Many of my patients are surprised to hear that shame also has a pretty clear-cut survival advantage. Shame warns us that we are at risk of being thrown out of the tribe—and anyone who is ostracized in that way is going to find it harder to survive. At one time, shame may have been literally about immediate survival: being in with the "in" crowd meant we could huddle together for warmth, for example, versus trying to last through a pre–central heating February on our own. And feelings of shame about adultery or some such transgression might prevent us from violating the tribe's norms, lest we be sent packing. (Or shame might encourage us to hide what we have done!)

Most of us no longer need others at such a basic level in order to survive. But we are still social creatures, and many benefits come to those who form strong connections with others. Today, shameful feelings may help protect our important relationships by deterring us from lying or cheating, for example. Shame can also serve as a beacon, highlighting what *not* to do and helping to keep us on a right path.

ANGER

Anger is also a warning sign that promotes safety and survival. Perhaps even more important, anger provides a motivating force. In evolutionary terms, feeling angry about someone stealing stored food helped ensure that our ancestors took action to rectify that situation. A Neanderthal who was too laid-back about such an affront would have had a very long, hungry winter—and had he survived it, he'd have had little with which to attract a mate or support offspring.

Today, anger might not keep you alive that directly very often, but it still helps you get up and *do* something to take care of what is valuable to you. It helps make sure people don't take advantage of you. Anger at your partner for treating you poorly one too many times might spur you to break up a relationship that is dragging you down. Anger at another person could also protect a relationship that is important to you, letting you know that something is awry and giving you a chance to fix it.

SADNESS

Sadness is a bit complicated to appreciate as contributing to survival, yet like anger, sadness can serve to protect what matters most to us. Sadness is triggered when we feel the loss of something important; therefore, it also serves to make us better appreciate what we have when we have it and to take better care of what we have to guard against its loss. For our ancestors, this may have had a direct cause and effect: sadness at the failure of a crop might have inspired more hours spent in the field the next time around, leading to a bumper crop and the ability to feed more children. Today we might feel sad at being passed over for promotion or over a breakup; we might then redouble our efforts to be worthy of a raise or relationship.

JEALOUSY

Jealousy is another example of an emotion with a more complicated role in evolutionary survival—and a modern benefit. Jealousy makes sure that we are interested in getting our fair share and that we are careful with our resources and don't take them for granted. A twinge of jealousy at seeing a woman chat up your husband at a party—demonstrating how she values him (or, in any case, his conversational contributions)—might remind you about what *you* value about him and inspire you to show it more.

DISGUST

Disgust, as well as its ability to keep us alive and reproducing as much as possible, has clear biological roots—for example, disgust is a very helpful response to rotten food or germy messes. If maggoty flesh made us feel *hungry*, say, our ancestors would probably have eaten their way into fatal disease long before they got around to begetting the next generation in the line that eventually led to us. Here's a fun fact about disgust: The associated facial expression is instantly understood across all cultures on the planet. Everyone, everywhere, will recognize that "eeeewwww!" look and know just what you mean, no matter where you are or where you come from.

LOVE AND HAPPINESS

Positive emotions have benefits too, of course—both personal and evolutionary. What living in Wise Mind helps us manage is their potential for *negative* effects. There's a reason we call it "lovesick." Rapid heartbeat, queasy stomach, neglect of necessary tasks—with emotion friends like these, who needs enemies?

Good feelings generally *are* good, but there are two basic ways in which they tend to go bad. One is when we don't get enough of them. We don't have enough experiences of love and happiness, and when we do, they don't last long enough. The second love/happiness booby trap is that of being amped up on positive feelings, which can lead us to make dumb choices. In our excitement, we get careless. In our joy, we can't see the downsides. We love blindly, so we trust the untrustworthy. We get so caught up in doing what we love that we don't take care of other things we need to attend to.

Within these two categories, we humans have a lot of substrategies for being bad at feeling good. We misunderstand what constitutes feeling good, overlook opportunities for feeling good, focus on how often we lack good feelings rather than how often we have them, and neglect to create good feelings for ourselves. We carry negative feelings into happy circumstances and allow them to win the day. We let the small stuff get us down, when we'd do better to look at the big picture, and we hope for big things to happen, when we'd do better to appreciate the little things we already have. We get so wrapped up in or carried away by positive emotions that we make decisions that don't seem like such a good plan when the buzz is over. We chase love and happiness as if we can or should have positive emotions only and always. We mistake instant gratification for happiness. We love when we get no love in return.

Managing negative emotions means (in part) seeking out the good within the bad; managing positive emotions means avoiding the bad while retaining the good. You need Wise Mind just as much in both types of situations. Living in Wise Mind can help you both increase the amount of love and happiness you experience *and* steer clear of poor choices while you are under the influence.

 WISE MIND LIVING PRACTICE
If You're Happy and You Notice It . . .

The easiest way to experience more positive emotions is to simply notice the love and happiness already in your life. One way of doing this is to look for the small things you might let fly by without appreciating them. This is a mash-up of the "take time to smell the roses" and "count your blessings" schools of thought. When you push the button for the elevator and—*bing!*—it opens right away, pay attention to the little huzzah that goes through you because you don't have to wait. (See, I mean *really* small things.) If everyone in your family sits down to dinner together at the same time for once, gather in that warm feeling. Savor the compliments you get. Appreciate the long-overdue conversation with a good friend. Take note of how you feel upon the successful completion of a tough task. Highlight for yourself any and all good, happy moments. Identify them. Specify to yourself all the happy details. *Notice.*

This is a kind of mindfulness practice. Although it focuses on the small, the rewards are great. As you practice, you will instantly feel happier and more loved and loving. We all have instances of love or happiness every day, even in the midst of our worst times; the trick is to claim them as they come to us. Some people keep a gratitude journal for this purpose; this is a wonderful way to remind yourself of all the good things you feel, especially when the going gets tough. Some families make it a point to hear a good thing from each member at some time during the day: maybe during a toast at dinner or a bedtime prayer or meditation. Whether or not you write down your moments of positive emotion, whether or not you share them with anyone, the power comes from just keeping them in mind.

BAD FEELINGS FOR GOOD REASONS

There's value even in painful emotions. Bad feelings exist for good reasons. They help you adapt to life's challenges, protect and defend yourself, respond to threat or loss, get motivated, and connect to others. Blocking bad feelings—well, *trying* to block bad feelings—will always end up making things worse. For one thing, it can't, in fact, be done. For another, you sacrifice the benefits you glean from emotions if you have nothing to balance them or to move you past them. The effort involved in denying an emotion is stressful in and of itself—often it is worse than bearing the full weight of the emotion. Using Wise Mind Living strategies, you can extract the good from the bad and avoid the bad in the good—or minimize the bad while maximizing the good. That's what managing your emotions is all about.

6

CHANGE HOW
YOU FEEL . . .

By Changing *What* You Feel

For months, Wanda had been having episodes where, all of a sudden, her heart raced so badly she was short of breath—so badly she felt she was *dying*. Wanda was sure her symptoms stemmed from an undetected heart condition of some dreadful kind. Her doctor reassured her she was in good general health, but Wanda insisted on a full heart workup.

It wasn't until all those expensive tests turned up absolutely nothing wrong with the physiology of her heart that Wanda could accept that perhaps the origin of the physical feelings she was having was not in her anatomical heart at all. With official data on the fitness of her heart, she was able to begin to recognize these episodes for what they were: panic attacks—feelings of anxiety (fear) writ large. This emotion demonstrates, in overly dramatic fashion, just how fundamentally physiological emotions are. And here's the kicker: because Wanda was in Emotion Mind as these symptoms occurred, she couldn't access her best analytical abilities to understand her symptoms and what they signified, much less make an effective plan for handling them. For that, she was going to need to be in Wise Mind.

Wanda's "heart problem" is an especially rowdy example of how emotions always reveal themselves, in large part, through physical signs. The symptoms may not tell you which emotion, exactly, is in the house, since there is much overlap in what happens to the body when you are anxious or excited or mad (such as flushed cheeks or an elevated heart rate). But once you know how to look, you will see a clear pattern indicating that you are in an emotional state. To tune in to *how* you are feeling emotionally, first spin the dial to awareness of *what* you are feeling physically.

Once you identify your physical feelings and the emotional feelings connected to them, you'll be prepared to move on to getting a handle on what's going on with your thoughts (see chapter 7) and behavior (see chapter 8). This is the triumvirate of change strategies—body, mind, and actions—that Wise Mind Living employs to alter the strategies that aren't serving you. The other side of the coin is acceptance strategies (see chapter 9) for coping with what you can't change. All of these elements are predicated on your first calming the emotional alarm bell going off in your body so you can respond rather than simply react.

When you are in Emotion Mind, your body is always activated. So the first step to regulating your emotions must be to tame the storm going on in your central nervous system. Calming the symptoms of emotional upset doesn't mean the emotions go away, but it can bring down the intensity of the experience. With the immediate chaos quieted, you can collect your wits and figure out what to do. You can return to being in Wise Mind.

Distressing emotions light up your autonomic nervous system, just as any stress does. (If you want to refresh your memory, check out the list of the common symptoms in "Signals of Emotion" on page 60.) Here's what happens: your heart rate goes up, you breathe faster, your muscles tense, and you sweat. There are also other changes that are less easy to see, though you might ultimately feel their effects just the same: your blood pressure goes up, your body releases stress hormones, your normal hormone balance is disrupted, your metabolism increases, your digestion slows, and your blood flow shifts to direct blood toward the brain and the major muscles needed for survival (and away from "nonessential" functions, such as warming your hands). All of your senses are heightened. And here's a big one that's often overlooked: your higher-order brain functions slow. Problem solving, learning, empathy, connection, flexible thinking—everything not deemed crucial for immediate survival goes straight out the window. Your attention becomes fixed and narrow. This is the physiological state that produces Emotion Mind, and it is very easy to get really stuck here; your body is conspiring to block your access to the tools of Wise Mind Living. That's why it is important to learn to read the physical pattern as a cue to recognizing, "Hey, I'm in Emotion Mind, here." This insight allows you to begin to break the hold that Emotion Mind has on you.

TRANSFORM YOUR HEALTH

Calming the physical effects of distressing emotions is important to your physical, mental, and emotional health. The ability to reach Wise Mind is key, of course. Another reason to get the physical effects of emotion under control is their effect on the cycle of emotion. If distressing emotions are left unmanaged, if physical symptoms are still there to be a part of the aftereffects of an emotional experience, they can be enough to retrigger the emotion. The trigger becomes internal rather than external. If you don't want the whole emotional experience to turn into a vicious cycle, you have to find an off-ramp somewhere, and taking care of physical symptoms is a great way to do that. If you don't take care of them—and if they therefore keep retriggering the same emotion—then you'll end up in a mood.

There's another argument to be made for nipping the physical symptoms of emotion in the bud: the simple truth is that when you lessen the headaches and jitters and muscle tension, you'll feel better. Without so much of your energy diverted into making you feel lousy, you'll find you will have many more resources to devote to whatever comes up in your life, good and bad, allowing you to maximize the one and minimize the other.

Longer-term outcomes are at stake, too. Physical responses from emotions can cause or lead to real health problems. Research shows that psychological factors and emotional states can play a large role in the development, progression, and outcome of some medical conditions, including cardiovascular disease (the most intensively studied in this regard) and cancer. The stress of distressing emotions can weaken the immune system and accelerate aging. Nearly two-thirds of all visits to primary care physicians are prompted by stress-related symptoms, including the stress of distressing emotions. Using Wise Mind Living strategies to manage your emotions can save you from a lot of trips to the doctor's office, as well as from a lot of heartache of a less concrete kind.

LIVING IN WISE MIND

"These Headaches Are Really Stressing Me Out"

Juliana came to see me as a sort of last resort. She suffered from terrible headaches and had been making the rounds of various doctors for more than a year to try to get some relief. No one she'd consulted had been able to offer treatments that stopped the headaches or even to pinpoint what was wrong. Finally she decided all that was left was learning to cope, somehow, with being in pain almost every day. The fierce and frequent headaches were really stressing her out, she explained, leaving her overwhelmed and depressed. If it weren't for the headaches, she felt that she wouldn't be such an emotional mess.

Spoiler alert! Juliana had it backward: her emotions were causing her physical symptoms, not the other way around. But to get to the point where she could see that for herself, she first had to calm her body. Who can think straight with a pounding headache? (And with a dinosaur brain in charge of your body!)

As she worked her way around to that switch in thinking, two strategies helped Juliana right off the bat. One was getting some exercise. She'd pretty much given it up as her physical symptoms got worse, but she decided to try doing some low-key movement several days a week. It didn't take long for her to detect a pattern: she felt better on the days she went walking than when she didn't.

The second key thing for Juliana was relaxation techniques. She set out to try relaxation as a way to ease her mind when she stressed about feeling bad, which had been her original way of thinking about her symptoms ("Having these headaches is stressing me out!"). She already recognized that stressing out about the headaches was only making her feel worse. So Juliana decided to take a bath every evening, a trick she already knew had helped her unwind on occasion. Now she added some slow-breathing exercises while in the tub to increase the relaxation effect. She also learned a basic guided relaxation sequence she could run through while she soaked. The relaxation brought immediate relief, and she said she always felt better after a bath. Soon she noticed not only that the relaxation exercises relieved her symptoms, but also that the effect seemed to carry forward, preventing, or at least delaying, their reappearance.

As she began feeling better, Juliana was ready to learn to accurately identify her emotions. For her, that began with learning to recognize when she was, in fact, having an emotional response. She had not quite been getting the message her body was sending out—the headaches, of course, but that wasn't all. When she was having an emotional response, she also experienced cold sweats, rapid heartbeat, and so on. Now, just being able to tell herself, "Oh, something has upset me," as she felt her body's response to an emotional trigger was enough to moderate the experience. She was then able to pull in her Wise Mind Living skills right in the midst of an emotion—usually by doing slow breathing at first—to better rein it in. Juliana would then use a Wise Mind Review to carefully label her emotion. Over time, she discovered that the emotion that popped up more than anything else was anxiety.

As she accepted this new perspective, she learned to think, "Feeling anxious is giving me a headache" instead of "I am so anxious about these headaches." Then she could deploy the practical interventions that would lessen her symptoms. As a result, her headaches abated in frequency and intensity. Soon she was having more "good" days (days without headaches). And with fewer headaches, she told me, she felt less stressed out. "Really, I feel less anxious," she corrected herself. And with less anxiety, her emotional state triggered headaches less often, so she was no longer "primed" for them as she once had been.

Juliana still got anxious sometimes, of course, and she still had other work to do (as you'll see in the next chapter), but she felt better prepared to do it once she felt she had a grip on how she felt physically. Even if she couldn't get rid of feeling sick altogether, she was confident that she at least had the tools to help her manage it when she did. ⚭

To keep the body in good health is a duty. . . .
Otherwise we shall not be able to keep our mind strong and clear.

BUDDHA

REDUCING YOUR VULNERABILITY

The most basic way of all to protect yourself from distressing emotions is to reduce your vulnerability to them. All of the ways you do that optimize your physical health, as well. You've heard all of this before, but what you may not know is that what I describe here is just as important to your mental and emotional health as it is to your physical health.

You have likely already experienced the connection. Think of a time when you didn't get much sleep or subsisted on junk food all day. How much more likely were you to get into a fight with your partner? Or be more upset by that fight than you might otherwise have been? That's it in a nutshell. When your body doesn't feel well, you are much more likely to feel bad emotionally.

A body in fine feather is an asset in handling any emotional experience. No matter what you are facing emotionally, you take your body with you into that situation. Whether you are navigating a contentious meeting with your boss, trying to manage a tantrumming child, giving a speech, or whatever else, if your body is at the top of its game, it can support you. If it's not, it may undermine you instead. You want your body to be physically calm so you can think through the situation and best handle whatever comes up.

To best set yourself up to stay out of Emotion Mind—and have easier access to Wise Mind—you should take good care of your body.

Balanced Eating

Eat regularly. Choose food wisely. Select sensible serving sizes. Not eating enough can cause moodiness and irritability. Skipping breakfast, for example, can cause a dip in blood sugar, which is one of the most common reasons for midmorning crankiness.

Exercise

Exercise is an excellent stress reliever. Not only does active exercise lead to greater muscle relaxation and increased production of antistress chemicals; research also shows that people who are physically fit exhibit less extreme physiological response to stress than their less-fit counterparts. This means physically fit people are less likely to experience the health problems linked with chronic stress. (Just don't overdo it.) Exercise that is actually relaxing while you do it, such as yoga or tai chi, induces a parasympathetic nervous system response that is incompatible with intense levels of emotion.

Balanced Sleep

Not too little sleep, but also not too much. When you don't get enough sleep, your body produces extra stress hormones. But too much sleep causes problems of its own. Most people need an average of eight hours a night.

Treat Any Physical Illness

Do routine maintenance—checkups and the like (including with the dentist). Take time to heal when you are injured or sick; there's no value in pushing through, no matter what.

Limit Mood-Altering Substances

This includes alcohol and tobacco. Here are a couple of common myths you should eliminate from your worldview:

> "A drink relaxes me and helps me sleep." *Alcohol actually interferes with healthy sleep cycles.*

> "Smoking is how I get rid of stress." *The chemicals that smoking pours into you activate your nervous system rather than calm it.*

HOW TO CHANGE WHAT YOU FEEL

No matter how well you care for your physical self, emotions are still going to happen, and they are still going to be heralded by physiological signals, many of which are not delightful. But you have an amazing ability to control that process, even though it happens lightning fast and deep within your brain. And you can develop that ability—*if* you practice. And you must practice not while you are in turmoil but when things are relatively calm, day in and day out, until you get good enough to give it a go in the heat of the moment. You have to practice when you are *not* in Emotion Mind so it'll be possible to do it when you *are*.

Physical responses to emotion are automatic (why do you think they call it the autonomic nervous system?). In the midst of the havoc of the immediate moment, the only part you can really control is breathing. This is why reaching Wise Mind often begins with a breathing exercise. If you can slow your breathing, you can create a cascade of positive effects, interrupting the cascade of negative effects. Slowing your breathing can slow your heartbeat, normalize hormone release, release tense muscles, and so on. Even if the signals of emotional upset come on automatically, you have this one switch that you can flip to turn them off: your breath. (You can also intentionally change the level of muscle tension, though it is harder to do on the spot. We will get to those relaxation exercises in a bit.)

Put on a Happy Face

Your body—your movements and expressions—can actually create, as well as express, emotional feelings. Activating the muscles that create an expression on your face triggers other, more internal, activations that create the mood that matches the expression. So if you frown, you'll feel mad—or sad, if it's a little frown. But smile and you'll feel happy. You can take your guidance on this from science and its "facial feedback hypothesis."

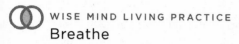

WISE MIND LIVING PRACTICE
Breathe

To calm your body in the midst of an emotional reaction, slow your breathing by extending your exhale. Focusing on the exhale is important because increasing the inhale can amount to hyperventilation.

Breathe in through your nose (to ensure you don't gulp air, which is easy to do when you are worked up), then out through your mouth, counting slowly to five. As you reach five, it should feel like you have fully exhaled. If you need to start with a count of three or four and build up to five, that's fine; it can take a few cycles to find a comfortable rhythm. If it seems difficult for your first few breaths, don't let that throw you. If your exhale is getting longer, you are doing it right.

WISE MIND LIVING PRACTICE
Relax Your Muscles

The quickest way to encourage a bit of relaxation while your body is in the grip of an emotional response is simply to think about releasing tensed muscles while you slow your breathing (see "Wise Mind Living Practice: Breathe," above). With each exhale, imagine your muscles softening. You might pick a few areas that you know need tending to—most people know where they tend to tighten up—and target those: inhale, exhale, and release your jaw; inhale, exhale, and release your neck and shoulders; inhale, exhale, and release your abdomen; and so on.

WISE MIND LIVING PRACTICE
Progressive Relaxation

When you are *not* smack in the middle of an emotional response, you should practice releasing all the muscles in your whole body with a basic progressive relaxation exercise. Get into a comfortable sitting or reclining position and close your eyes. You might want to begin by doing a quick inventory of where your body is holding tension. Is there any place in particular that doesn't feel relaxed? Any place muscles are active or working for unidentifiable purposes? Any place you feel like your muscles are trying to hold you up even though you are otherwise fully supported?

You may want to spend a few extra moments on any problem areas you identified, but then be sure to move through your entire body, regardless, toes to head, tensing and releasing one group of muscles at a time. Tense your toes; then release them. Flex your feet; then let them go again. Keep going with your calves, thighs, and so on, right up to your head. (Tense up your face; then release. Can you tense your scalp muscles? Are there muscles in your scalp?)

Once you have finished tensing and releasing all the muscle groups you can think of, allow yourself to remain in a state of relaxation for at least a few more minutes before you end the exercise.

When you do progressive relaxation, you are using the basic physiology of muscle fibers to your advantage: when you work (tense) a muscle fiber, it is then able to stretch (relax) more afterward. Experiencing the difference between tension and relaxation helps you get to a deeper sense of relaxation; you'll feel the contrast mentally as well as physically. And actively creating the change you are feeling, over and over, gives you more of a sense of control over your body's reactions.

It is not always easy to release your muscles on purpose. Enlist your brain to send a signal to your body to let go of tension. Try using different images or suggestions to see what successfully triggers relaxation: imagine things getting heavier or warmer or looser. Or imagine them floating. A little trial and error should be all you need to find out what works best for you.

There is more wisdom in your body than in your deepest philosophy.
FRIEDRICH NIETZSCHE

BODY SCAN

The basic Mindfulness Body Scan (page 29) has a few handy variations that are useful for changing how you feel. I hope that you've been practicing mindfulness in some relatively serene moments so that now you'll be ready to take it into the heat of an emotional reaction. You might not really be able to do this variation while a triggering event is happening (you probably can't go lie down to concentrate this way while you're in the middle of an argument with someone), but when you get to a time and space where you can work on this, give it a try. Eventually, you'll get practiced enough that you can more or less do this on the fly, though it takes quite a bit of experience to build up to that.

 WISE MIND LIVING PRACTICE
Mindfulness Body Scan (A Variation)

One way to use the scan is as a mindfulness practice to become aware of the physical signs you are experiencing. But keep in mind, you are just to observe them, not change them. Simply do a scan, toe to head, with a focus on physical sensation. Get detailed: "What does this little bit of me feel like right now?" Look for the signs of distressing emotions outlined earlier in this chapter, but also include every little thing you can feel. Notice the points of contact between your body and the floor or chair, how and where your clothing touches your skin, and which muscles are working. Note any slight tingling you feel as you bring attention to an area. You can actually increase blood flow to an area by concentrating on it, and you might even be able to feel the nerves waking up as a result.

When you do a body scan while emotion alarm bells are going off, you can practically hear your own heartbeat. You'll *feel* it for sure: "My heart is thumping!" You're also sure to feel muscle tension, perhaps in your chest or the back of your neck. As always, you should also attend to your breathing—in this case, the physical feeling of it.

As discussed, this scan alone can be powerful and enlightening, without even attempting to use it to change how you feel. But after beginning with the traditional Mindfulness Body Scan (page 29), you can then build on it: During your body scan, as you identify sensations you'd like to soothe or eliminate, see what you can do in the moment to facilitate that. Can you slow your breathing? Can you release muscle tension?

Essentially, you want to combine some of the breathing and relaxation practices you learned earlier with the body scan. It isn't always easy, especially when your emotional physiology is activated, to get a grip on what is happening in your body. And if you are not very clear on what exactly is happening, it is hard to know what to do about it. So when you have the time and ability to do the body scan, it's a helpful addition to the earlier practices.

(For the record, when you begin to work on changing what you find, you've technically left the realm of classical mindfulness, which would not have you purposefully interfere with what is observed.)

HOW WISE MIND LIVING IS LIKE WEIGHT LIFTING

As you would with any body-building program, you have to invest some time with these exercises if you want to see results. Your best bet is to commit to something specific about how and when you will practice—scheduling a time with yourself (actually putting it on your calendar) or tying it to a particular event in your day increases the odds that you'll really do it. For example, you might decide to do a relaxation exercise every night when you get in bed, at the end of every day at work before you turn off your computer, or every day before you leave your desk to go for lunch. By scheduling a time, you'll be more likely to actually do it than if you just have a vague notion of trying a relaxation exercise sometime.

No matter how much you practice, you can't get rid of every headache with these strategies. And I don't mean to suggest you can breathe your way to eliminating all anger or fear or relax your way to solving all your problems. But when you calm your physical responses to distressing emotions, you'll be moving toward Wise Mind Living—and the ability to master your emotions. It's very hard to be wise if your heart is beating double time or your stomach's tied in knots.

7

CHANGE HOW
YOU FEEL . . .

By Changing What You *Think*

What you think is how you feel. Something happens, you (and your brain) make an interpretation of what happened, and boom, there you are, having an emotion. That's the cycle of emotion. We've been breaking down this cycle into component parts, and as you know, the thoughts at the interpretation stage are absolutely key to how you experience the emotion. Some thoughts come instantaneously, like an advance guard of Emotion Mind. But the Emotion Mind ideas that pop into your head often do not want to be bothered with the facts. They are not, on the whole, optimists. They cannot be relied upon to present a logical or objective case. They are prone to unrealistically distorting your experiences. This is the way your thoughts can cause, exacerbate, or sustain distress.

The thoughts you develop over time as you replay or reflect on what happens matter too—how you think through something, how you explain it to yourself, what you make of it, and what sticks with you. This is where you can most readily make changes. You can't really stop a thought from popping into your head, but whether it takes root, is weeded out, or gets bonsai-ed into a more desirable, lasting shape depends on you.

Remember, too, that this is a cycle, so *how you feel is what you think* is just as true as *what you think is how you feel.* Your overall mood and earlier emotional experiences influence your interpretation of and your thoughts about whatever happens. If you are already in a negative place, you will interpret whatever happens negatively: count this among the reasons it is important to manage your emotions and the cycle of emotion, so that you don't arrive at the aftereffects stage in a state of mind that launches you straight back into another round of distress.

The *good* news is that your thoughts can also help you avoid or curtail emotional distress. You can change your thoughts and your pattern of thoughts; and in doing so, you can change how you feel and how you experience emotion. Which way it goes is up to you. You may be able to muddle through if you rely on Logic Mind, but your analysis will be incomplete. It's also all too easy to get stuck in negative patterns of thinking and therefore in negative experiences of emotion: Emotion Mind. By using Wise Mind through the cycle of emotion—that is, by taking a mindful view and being nonjudgmental, balanced, and compassionate—you can chart a course away from distress and toward happiness.

CREATE YOUR OWN HEALING

Juliana, the woman with unrelenting headaches who learned that emotions were behind her physical symptoms, created her own healing by changing her thoughts. Her essential switch—from "I am anxious about feeling sick" to "My anxiety is making me feel sick"—was just as important to feeling better as were getting more exercise and practicing relaxation techniques. As she shifted her thoughts, she not only experienced a decrease in physical symptoms but also cleared some mental and emotional space that allowed her to dig deeper into her thoughts and emotions and resolve her problem—not only on the surface but also at the root. Using the Wise Mind Review (page 45) and the Wise Mind Debate (coming up!), she soon identified a pattern: her mind's "default" setting, it seemed, was to consider herself to blame for whatever went wrong, whether or not there was evidence for this. If she called a friend and the friend didn't call her back the same day, she thought, "I must have done something to upset her." If her boss praised someone else's project in a meeting, Juliana thought, "She must not really like me." If she had to ask to extend a deadline, Juliana thought, "I'm no good at this work."

This wasn't anything she'd ever paused to consider before. But when she did examine her thinking, she easily compiled alternative interpretations and contrary evidence that pointed to a more balanced view of the situations. Instead of fearing for her job over every little thing, she learned to rely on her long history of good work as the most important contribution to her job security. And she recognized that, logically, her friend probably just hadn't picked up the call yet, or it had slipped her mind, or she'd been too busy to call back but would eventually. When negative feelings (physical and emotional) started up, she could "catch" herself—"There I go again, thinking it *must* be my fault, when I don't really know what is going on"—and adjust her thought process. The more she did that, the less often the troublesome feelings came up.

GET READY, GET SET, . . .

Just like Juliana, you are going to have to lay a little groundwork before you are ready to work directly on changing your thoughts. Luckily, you've already been practicing mindfulness, so you have your most important tool honed and ready to go. Mindfulness is a component of all the practices in this chapter, even the ones that don't seem meditative at all. But the ability to focus on your thoughts and the emotions they create and reflect is a big part of *why* you learned mindfulness. By using the sequence described in this section, you will be able to use mindfulness to pay attention to your thoughts, identify what they actually are, discover how often you are thinking them, look for patterns, and evaluate their appropriateness and accuracy. Then you'll be ready to figure out where you want to intervene and how best to go about it.

Calm Down

Often the very first step to changing your thoughts is to calm your body by engaging in some of the practices covered in chapter 6. Other times you may need to take action first (or successfully *not* take an unproductive or harmful action), as will be discussed in chapter 8. But remember: you do not want to try working with your thoughts while you are in Emotion Mind or otherwise really wound up. When emotion is intense, your thoughts are too "hot" to handle, and you need to let them—and you—cool off a bit before you begin. So when you need to, take a literal or metaphorical walk around the block *before* getting down to business.

You can't go wrong by doing five minutes of Mindfulness of Breath (page 26) before beginning any of the exercises in this chapter. Being present for a little while can be calming, and it clears some mental clutter to create open space for working with your thoughts. (That space is Wise Mind.) Warming up your nonjudgmental stance is also another plus.

Sit with It

You are also going to have to identify and acknowledge your emotions so that you can change them by changing your thoughts. In chapter 9, you will learn more about the importance of just experiencing the feelings you are having (see "Wise Mind Living Practice: Mindfulness of Emotion," page 146). But in essence, you just sit there and allow yourself to feel your feelings. Go ahead and feel sad or scared or angry or whatever it is you are feeling, abandoning for just a little while the problematic quest to somehow escape or avoid your feelings. You don't really have to know any more about this step to give it a try. That simple form of acknowledgment that you are feeling an emotion is what you are after right now. Sometimes experiencing your emotion fully is enough to restore balance. But even if it is just the beginning of the process, and not a solution in and of itself, it has a healing effect.

Pin It Down

Identifying your thoughts is just as important as identifying your emotion—assuming you aim to change either one. It may be worthwhile to review "Common Interpretations" (page 64), which contains common thoughts by the emotions they are linked to. Another way to clarify just what you were and are thinking is to answer some basic questions about the event that set this emotional experience in motion. The following questions are invaluable clarifiers:

"What's the first thing that went through my mind when this happened?"

"What am I thinking about it now? What am I telling myself about it?"

"What is so upsetting about this?"

"What memories did this stir up?"

"What do I think this says about me? My life? My future?"

"What do I think this makes others think about me?"

"What does this tell me about another person or about people in general?"

"What am I worried might happen now?"

WHAT WERE YOU THINKING?

It can be hard to see habitual patterns of unhelpful thinking; you often engage in them without thinking about them. So when you *do* actually try to pay attention to your unhelpful thought patterns, it can be a little challenging. It is helpful to know some of the most common patterns that distort thinking, because there are bound to be some that seem pretty familiar. Once you learn to recognize the pattern, it becomes easier to find anything in your own thoughts that matches it. I am sure you are a very original person, but the sad fact is that when it comes to thinking about emotional experiences, you get tripped up in the same ways everyone else does.

Unhelpful patterns of thought and interpretation are more likely to pop up the more stressed or distressed you are. These exaggerated, irrational patterns are brought to you by Emotion Mind—no surprise there. Most of us jump right to one or two of these distorted patterns of thinking—we probably all use all of them at one time or another, but everyone will have his or her own go-to patterns that are favored above all others. The most popular patterns are discussed here.

Black-and-White Thinking

The more stressed out you are, the more likely you are to think in absolutes. Life is either totally awesome or a complete train wreck. There are no shades of gray, not even one—no room for complexity in people or situations.

You might be an all-or-nothing kind of thinker if . . . you have never met a summary sentence that does not deserve an "always" or "every" or "never" in it. Remember, there is no middle ground!

Jumping to Conclusions

This comes in two flavors: mind reader and forecaster. Both are very popular ways to stress yourself out. You can do it in one easy step: draw conclusions about a situation without knowing all the facts . . . or, heck, any facts. Be sure to assume something negative, and don't let lack of evidence stand in your way. You can infer someone else's thoughts and feelings and motivations; you are especially good at knowing exactly how someone is feeling about you. But don't ask *them* about it, or you won't be mind reading! You can also predict the outcome (almost always negative) of things that haven't happened yet: "They are not going to hire me—there is no point to going on this interview."

You might be a conclusion jumper if . . . "I just know he didn't call because he doesn't like me" seems like a good explanation to you.

Catastrophizing

This is barely a word, but you know what it means anyway: there's nothing that happens that you cannot construe as a catastrophe. You tell yourself the absolute worst *will* happen or that a situation is horrific and intolerable. You are very, very good at worst-case scenarios. No doubt that's where you're headed! There's often a mountain-out-of-a-molehill aspect to this. Wise Mind reflection might reveal the impending catastrophe to be not only not as bad as all that, but also not as big.

You might be a catastrophizer if . . . you have a disagreement with your spouse, and now you are worried you're going to end up divorced.

Overgeneralizing

One piece of evidence—that's all you need. From there, it's easy enough to draw a conclusion: a hasty, unreliable conclusion, drawn as it is from insufficient evidence and inadequate experience.

You might be an overgeneralizer if . . . one person turns you down for a date, and you think, "I'm such a loser."

Unrealistic Expectations

You are all about the *musts* and *shoulds*. Then when you, someone else, or life in general tends not to measure up to these uncompromising rules, you are left feeling guilty, angry, frustrated, or resentful. You end up blaming yourself and others for things that aren't under your (or their) control.

You might hold unrealistic expectations if . . . you believe *shoulds* should be all the motivation anyone needs.

Discounting the Positive

This is a special form of negativity. Not only do you focus on and magnify the negative aspects of a person, situation, or experience, but you also filter out any and all positives—or treat them as if they simply don't count.

You might be discounting the positive if . . . you receive a compliment or congratulations and chalk it up to mere flattery.

Emotional Reasoning

Emotional reasoning is when you believe your emotions are facts and that your feelings reflect the way things actually are. "If I feel this way, then it must be true"—that's your motto.

You might be an emotional reasoner if . . . you feel stupid after making a boneheaded mistake and then conclude that you are, when you get down to brass tacks, actually stupid.

Personalization

Everything is about you—or at least all the bad things are. You are sure that anything negative is directed at you or that you are responsible for it happening.

You might be a personalizer if . . . when your boss reschedules a meeting to a time that inconveniences you, you figure, "He did that just to annoy me."

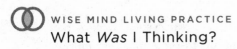

WISE MIND LIVING PRACTICE
What *Was* I Thinking?

The way to identify—and bust—unhelpful thinking is to do a partial Wise Mind Review (page 45), with particular focus (for now) on the interpretations part. For at least a week or so, you are going to use your Wise Mind Living journal to watch your thinking and look for patterns in it.

Over the course of the week, for any emotion you'd rate at least a four or five on a zero-to-ten scale (that is, any time you are feeling at least somewhat distressed), note in your journal the trigger and your interpretation. Identify what happened: the who, what, where, and when facts of the situation. Observe your interpretation of the situation. What did you think and feel?

Go ahead and throw in naming the emotion and write down the intensity (zero to ten). On all points, be specific. Try to make your journal entry about an emotion as close in time to the event as possible; if it can't be immediate, make sure to do it by the end of the day.

Write these journal entries with an eye toward finding any of the negative patterns described in the previous section. Do you see any distorted thinking? Sometimes just noticing it is enough to interrupt it: "Oh, look at me, jumping to conclusions again." (Of course, sometimes it's not enough. For those occasions, see "Wise Mind Living Practice: Wise Mind Debate," page 104.)

At the end of the week, look through the whole week's worth of journal entries for patterns across time. If you are finding distorted thoughts, like black-and-white thinking or catastrophizing, do you find that certain categories pop up more than others? Maybe you can discover a common trigger to several emotional reactions ("I am pretty touchy on days when I skip the gym" or "I got upset after all the times I spoke with my parents this week"). Do you see any habits of thought that are not working for you? When certain thoughts are part of a pattern, how often do they come up? Every day? Several times a day? Every hour? Just off the cuff, can you see any place where your thoughts might be creating or supporting distress?

> Anger is never without a reason, but seldom with a good one.
> BEN FRANKLIN

MAKE YOUR CASE

Sometimes just noticing that you are thinking in unhelpful patterns will open enough space for you to think more clearly. At other times, you may need to spend a bit of time creating an actual case to challenge a negative thought pattern in order to break it up, sweep it out, and make way for a more productive way of thinking. This is a Wise Mind Debate; next to mindfulness, it may be the most important Wise Mind Living tool you will learn. The Wise Mind Debate process works best when you do it in Wise Mind. However, you might need it most when you are *not* in Wise Mind. Fortunately, going through the debate process is also a good way to invoke Wise Mind if you are not quite there yet.

Specific directions for doing a Wise Mind Debate are up next, but let me first give you the basic outline of the process: You will begin by completing a partial Wise Mind Review, writing down your thoughts (the better to know what they actually are). Then, you will engage in a debate with yourself, identifying, challenging, and eventually weeding out any sketchy ways of thinking. Finally, you will create a new Wise Mind view of the situation.

In a Wise Mind Debate, your Wise Mind self is going to try to show your Emotion Mind self where it is getting it wrong. Your task is to assemble evidence about why your thoughts are *not* completely true. You'll take the thought distortions you reveal with your Wise Mind Living journal and argue against those as if you were a lawyer appearing before a really particular judge. The kind of judge who'll call out "Objection!" on behalf of your imaginary legal opponent. The kind of judge who is never going to let you get away with basing your case on opinions, hearsay, wishes, or anything other than facts. You'll need *proven* facts. Picking apart the illogic of emotional thinking this way can both free you from negative emotions and boost positive emotions.

"Wise Mind Living Practice: Wise Mind Debate" (page 104) includes a list of questions to help you with this process of challenging your thinking. You might also need to do a little information gathering. Check out the facts with someone else, for example. Ask for help if you can't think of a good or full argument. Remember that you are like a lawyer trying a case—which means you can call an expert witness! (You might even believe that witness more than you believe yourself.)

While we're on the topic of you-as-lawyer, imagine the other side presenting a good case, and then rebut it. Refine your case. If you don't buy your argument, neither will the judge or jury—which, in this case, is also you. The point is that for this to work, you really have to make your best case.

Wanda had a star witness who won her case for her. Remember Wanda and her racing heart and the expensive testing that finally proved her cardiovascular system was healthy and that therefore she was experiencing panic attacks rather than heart attacks? Wanda learned to do Wise Mind Debates as part of learning to deal with panic attacks. The medical testing was her ace in the hole whenever her old familiar (and extremely unhelpful) thought patterns popped up. Instead of slipping them on like comfortable old slippers, she called to the stand that medical report to give "just the facts, ma'am": "I just had my heart checked, and it is fine." Wanda went in for a high-tech checkup and came home with something much better than a diagnosis; she came home with a be-all, end-all answer for her Wise Mind Debates. Although effective debates do not always stop her panic attacks from coming, those attacks now seem a whole lot less scary. And the calmer Wanda can stay when they strike, the faster they go away, and the more confident she is in her ability to bear with them.

The final step of the Wise Mind Debate is to arrive at a more balanced Wise Mind way of looking at the situation. (Wanda's way: "These symptoms may be very unpleasant, but they are not going to kill me.") What does the evidence support? Be sure to write down your conclusion.

A Wise Mind Debate is not some Pollyanna, positive-thinking whitewash. The goal is never to simply replace negative thoughts with positive ones. That's unrealistic, for one thing, and you wouldn't even believe yourself anyway. Also, the negative interpretation may be the factually correct one. In order for it to work, a Wise Mind Debate must be based on evidence and rooted in reality. What you're after is not "thinking positive" but rather thinking in a more balanced and rational way; that's how you'll *feel* more balanced.

It is important to do these debates in writing because a lot of Emotion Mind thinking comes from a more creative, less rational part of the brain. Writing forces you to use another part of the brain and bring reason and logic into the mix. You'll also do a more thorough job of it if you do it in writing. Writing it down means that, by definition, you'll spend more time on the project. And writing exposes any halfhearted efforts; committing it to paper is committing to do the thing full-out.

Eventually, the process will become more automatic. The patterns revealed may allow you some shortcuts. For example, Gina got to the point where she could remind herself of the lessons she'd drawn from Wise Mind Debates, and that was enough. After a few months of written debates, Gina caught herself imagining all kinds of bad reasons a colleague had cut her off in a meeting. But she was able to tell herself, "Oh, there I go again, jumping to conclusions," and shift to a more realistic way of thinking it through, all without having to break out her notebook. Another patient, Deneen, has a Wise Mind Living journal full of musings about food. She's debated her various takes on the subject often enough that she's now able to quickly remind herself that "this cheesecake will make me happy" does not turn out to be reliably true. She no longer has to go through the whole written process every time she's faced with a pint of Ben and Jerry's ice cream.

◎ WISE MIND LIVING PRACTICE
Wise Mind Debate

To do a Wise Mind Debate, create the following subject headings in your Wise Mind Living journal:

> **Prompting Event**
> **Interpretation**
> **Unhelpful Thought Patterns**
> **Challenging Evidence**
> **More Balanced Interpretation**

Walk yourself through the situation, filling in information for each subject heading. Take as much space to do this as required—there is no set length; you may need a single sentence or a list of details, or it may be different for each situation.

Under "Prompting Event," write about what triggered your stress. Be sure to include the who, what, where, and when of the matter. Next, under "Interpretation," note your thoughts, beliefs, and assumptions about the situation. The questions in "Pin It Down" (page 96) may be helpful with this part.

Next, look for any negative patterns of thinking (review "What Were You Thinking?" on page 97 for clues) and note them under "Unhelpful Thought Patterns." You can decide whether you want to include the specific ideas in your head—but at least jot down the category (*catastrophizing*, etc.).

To fill in "Challenging Evidence," reread what you have written so far and see if you can identify any unhelpful thought patterns. Also note whether you would characterize any other thoughts as emotional thinking. Ask yourself, "Is that Emotion Mind talking?" Then write down statements that challenge any of these negative thoughts. Asking yourself the following questions should get you started:

> "Is there any other way to look at this?"
> "Is there any evidence that suggests that this way of
>   thinking isn't completely true?"

"Am I jumping to conclusions that aren't justified by
the evidence?"

"Am I focusing on my weaknesses and overlooking
my strengths?"

"What advice would I give to my best friend or a
loved one in this situation?"

"What would my best friend or a loved one say to
me about this situation?"

"What evidence might someone point out to show
me that my thoughts aren't completely accurate?"

"What have I learned from past experiences that
could help me now?"

"What have I done before to feel better about this?"

"Is this really as important as it seems right now? Will
I see this situation differently in two months, or two
years, than I do today? Will I even remember it?"

"Am I blaming myself for something I don't have
complete control over?"

"Am I blaming someone else for something they don't
have complete control over?"

For "More Balanced Interpretation," rewrite your thoughts about the
triggering event in a more balanced way, sticking to the facts.

If you like, you can rate the intensity of your emotion as you begin
the debate and then again at the conclusion to see how your feelings
might have changed as a result of the exercise.

You can make it a habit to do a Wise Mind Debate at the end of
the day before going to bed, working through whichever one or two
examples of being in Emotion Mind stand out most to you from the
day. Doing so is especially helpful for those times when you can't stop
thinking about something, to the point that it will literally keep you up
at night. Writing it down can help get it out of your head so you can
sort it out.

Some people can go on with Wise Mind Debates all day—challenging
every thought, filling up binders full of journal entries—but you don't

have to. You can pick what to focus on, choosing what's most troubling to you or what seems most likely to be resolvable.

Gina Challenges Herself

Gina did a Wise Mind Debate the day she walked into the office, said hello to her assistant, Theresa, and got no response. At her desk, she took out the notebook she had stashed in her purse for just such occasions. Here's what she wrote:

Prompting Event:
> T. didn't say anything when I said hello. My feelings are hurt!

Interpretation:
> 1. She's angry at me for something I did.
> 2. Now this is going to be a horrible day.

Unhelpful Thought Patterns:
> Jumping to conclusions
> Overgeneralizing

Challenging Evidence:
> - I don't remember doing anything that would have made T. angry.
> - T. might just be having a bad day.
> - T. might not have heard me when I said hello.
> - I've been looking forward to the team meeting today and my drinks date this evening, and T. doesn't have anything to do with those things.

More Balanced Interpretation:
> I have no idea why T. didn't say hello back. Instead of jumping to conclusions and feeling hurt, I will check this out with T. If she is mad, that won't be fun. But I can deal. None of this has to ruin my whole day. ◑

CORE BELIEFS: IS THAT A GREEN BANANA, OR ARE YOU JUST WEARING BLUE GLASSES?

There's another layer to the interpretations you make as part of the cycle of emotion. You (just like everybody else) are operating under the influence of a set of core beliefs, or deeply held views about yourself and the world. You use these underlying assumptions as shortcuts to understand the nature of your life and the world you live in. Your core beliefs comprise what you believe about yourself, what you believe about other people, and what you believe about the way the world works. So your core beliefs have quite a lot of input into your reactions to any given situation. Scratch a thought process or interpretation, and underneath you'll see core beliefs propping everything up. For better or worse!

Core beliefs act as filters in the making of your interpretations—everything passes through this set of assumptions on the way to forming your reactions to any given situation. Imagine wearing blue-tinted glasses. If you were presented with a perfectlsy ripe banana and asked what color it appeared to be, you'd say "green." If you weren't familiar with bananas or weren't aware of the color of your lenses, you would have full confidence that bananas are green.

If you were mindful of looking at the world through blue-colored glasses, however, you might see a green banana, but you would *know* it was actually yellow, since everything appears slightly blue to you. You would know that your filter had altered your perception, and you would then recognize what is true accordingly. Until you can identify the properties of the lens you are looking through, you can't adequately assess the facts of the matter.

Core beliefs are deeply ingrained in you, so you might not always recognize that you are wearing blue glasses. That's just fine as far as Emotion Mind is concerned, because it is right at home with a collection of questionable core beliefs. Living in Wise Mind, by contrast, means being aware of your filters. Awareness decreases the power of faulty filters, but not until you can see the filters (and not just see *through* them).

Wise Mind can help you uncover and evaluate your core beliefs and change your filters as necessary. You really need Wise Mind for that, because core beliefs feel like a part of you, of who you are. And because you need core beliefs (we all do), it doesn't feel comfortable to get rid of them. You need a way to understand yourself. You need a way to understand others. You need a worldview. But what you may have that you do *not* need are unhelpful, counterproductive, or even damaging core beliefs. Or, as commonly happens, core beliefs that were formed in another era of your life, perhaps for good reasons, but that no longer hold true and are getting in your way.

It is a lot harder to change a core belief than it is to change your other ways of thinking. Sometimes, though, that's exactly what you need to do if you have one (or more) that really isn't working for you. The process is essentially another Wise Mind Debate, but now the core-belief thoughts may be more stubborn. Fortunately, just identifying your core beliefs, without changing them or while change is still in process, can help quite a bit. If you know what your core beliefs are and which ones aren't helpful, then when a problematic one comes to the fore, you can notice it and remind yourself that you do not want to use a faulty belief such as that one. It's your core belief; you get to decide whether you will heed it.

Some kinds of therapy are all about how you arrived at your core belief, but I'm not a big fan of digging around until you unearth all the specific details to piece together the ultimate origin story. I *am*, however, very much in favor of figuring out more generally where it came from as a strategy for challenging it. It is true that core beliefs usually form during childhood, so identifying them may indeed mean poking around in your childhood a bit—just enough to see the source. You can then check to see whether what was important at that time is still relevant now. You have a chance to say to yourself, "Oh, so that's where that came from—but that's not true anymore. I don't have to let it affect me the same way now as it did then."

You may identify core beliefs by seeing themes emerge in your Wise Mind Living journal entries and Wise Mind Debates. Another clue that a core belief might be a faulty filter for your experiences is if you find yourself having a really hard time *believing* the more balanced Wise Mind view you've come up with in a debate. That's evidence of a core belief trying to detour you from Wise Mind; it's also a good sign that you have more work yet to be done in that area.

Having trouble with really stubborn core beliefs that are not serving you well is a good reason to try therapy. You may have some beliefs that you just can't budge on your own, not even with the help of a very wise book!

COMMON PROBLEMATIC CORE BELIEFS

Core beliefs are global, not situational. You don't automatically alter them based on the changing context of your life or your circumstances or your understanding. You hold them to be true all the time (with whether or not you should do so being an entirely separate matter!). You consider your core beliefs to be absolute and true, though you may not be conscious of doing so. One of the toughest things about problematic core beliefs is that because they filter your world for you, they also filter out evidence against them. If you proceed through the world with a core belief along the lines of "the world is a dangerous place," you are much more likely to find that the world *is* dangerous, or at least feels dangerous, because you focus on the threatening and overlook the reassuring.

Core beliefs are personal and idiosyncratic, but the ones that tend to cause problems generally follow a few common themes. If any of these ring a bell, you'll know which ones to look for in your Wise Mind Living journal entries.

Worthless

This one is at the top of the list because it comes up more than any other single category for my patients, and it drives a variety of problematic behaviors—most popularly, overeating and overspending. It's often behind depression. The core beliefs in this category reflect a general sense that one is inherently flawed, incompetent, or inferior.

"I'm worthless."
"I'm not good enough."
"I can't get anything right."

"I'm stupid."

"I'm a bad person."

"I'm unattractive (ugly, fat, etc.)."

"I'm useless."

"I'm a failure."

"I don't deserve anything good."

"There's something wrong with me."

"I'm always wrong."

"I've done things wrong."

"I'm damaged."

"Who do I think I am?"

"Other people are better than me."

"I'm a loser."

Unlovable

People who hold core beliefs about being unlovable often make the assumption that other people don't understand them and will not accept or approve of them. This theme often reflects an overemphasis on status, money, and achievement.

"I'm not lovable."

"I don't deserve love."

"I'm always left out."

"I'm not wanted."

"I'm alone."

"I'm unwelcome."

"I don't fit in anywhere."

"I'm uninteresting."

"Nobody loves me."

"I'm going to be rejected."

"I'm only worth something if people like me."

"It's important to be admired."

Distrustful

These core beliefs are typically rooted in abandonment. People who are distrustful often assume they will lose anyone to whom they form an emotional attachment. There may also be overlap with unlovable core beliefs.

"People are untrustworthy."
"I can't trust or rely on another person."
"People I love will leave me."
"I will be abandoned if I love or care for someone or something."
"I am uninteresting, and people will leave me because of it."
"I'm unimportant."
"I can't be happy if I'm on my own."
"I'm bound to be rejected/abandoned/alone."
"People will hurt me."
"People will let me down."

Helpless

This type of core belief generally results in people assuming they lack control and cannot handle anything effectively or independently. Individuals who believe they are helpless often face difficulties making changes. Furthermore, a sense of powerlessness can cause people to try to overcontrol their environment or to completely give up control.

"I'm helpless."
"I'm powerless."
"I'm out of control."
"I'm vulnerable."
"I'm trapped."
"I'm needy."
"I can't change."
"I can't handle anything."
"Other people will manipulate me and control my life."
"I can't do it."
"I can't stand up for myself."

"The world is a dangerous place."
"Bad things happen all the time."
"People will hurt me if I let them."

Superior

These core beliefs lead to a sense of entitlement, which can lead to rule breaking, resentment of others' success, and unreasonable demands that others must meet your needs. These beliefs may develop out of compensation for feeling defective or socially undesirable. They may not always be readily apparent.

"I'm superior and am entitled to special treatment
   and privileges."
"If people don't respect me, I can't stand it."
"I deserve a lot of attention and praise."
"If I don't excel, then I'm inferior and worthless."
"If I don't excel, I'll just end up ordinary."
"I am a very special person, and other people should treat
   me that way."
"I don't have to be bound by the rules that apply to
   other people."
"Other people should satisfy my needs."
"People have no right to criticize me."
"Other people don't deserve the good things that
   they get."
"People should go out of their way for me."
"People don't understand/get me because I am special/
   brilliant/etc."

Self-Sacrificing

These core beliefs may produce caretaking behavior, but it's the caretaking variety that forfeits your own needs in the service of others. People operating under these beliefs may feel guilty and compensate by putting the needs of others ahead of their own needs, believing they are responsible for the happiness of others. Here's a surefire sign: excessive apologizing.

"My needs are not important."
"It's not okay to ask for help."
"I have to do everything myself."
"If I don't do it, no one will."
"If I care enough, I can fix him/her/this."
"I shouldn't spend time taking care of myself."
"When I see that others need help, I have to
    help them."
"I'm only worthwhile if I'm helping other people."
"If I express negative feelings in a relationship,
    terrible things will happen."
"I have to make people happy."

Perfect

These core beliefs can masquerade as conscientiousness and a good strong work ethic. But on closer examination, it turns out to be taken too far. For people who hold these core beliefs, their sense of self-worth is often overly tied to external praise and accomplishments. They also tend to think in very black-and-white terms, hold rigid standards, and can be quick to discount positives. Perfectionists believe that they must strive to act and be at their best all the time in order to prove they are capable, worthy, and lovable.

"I have to do everything perfectly."
"If I make a mistake, it means I'm careless/a
    failure/etc."
"People who make mistakes should have negative
    consequences."
"People should behave properly or be punished if
    they don't."

Negative

These core beliefs are held by people we would all identify as pessimists. Their view of the world, themselves, and other people is always of the glass-half-empty variety. Beware of people who say, "I am not a pessimist; I am a realist," for they are often guided by one of these negativity core beliefs.

"Nothing ever works out for me."
"This world is falling apart."
"Life inherently sucks."
"Life is meaningless."

YOUR CORE BELIEFS ARE DEBATABLE

There are ways to work on changing your core beliefs, but they get pretty complicated pretty quickly. You might find that your work in this area is more suitable for therapy than a DIY model. But there's value in simply identifying your core beliefs—"Oh, I have to remember I'm wearing those blue glasses"—so you can hold them in your awareness, and *that* you can do on your own. You'll probably find some of these core beliefs simply by looking back through your Wise Mind Review and Wise Mind Debate journal entries. In the realm of thought patterns, what keeps coming up? What's causing problems? What's not working? The patterns you discern can point you toward what core beliefs may be lodged in your mind.

You can also do what is essentially a Wise Mind Debate, but with a core belief in place of an interpretation. You might do one based on a debate for an emotional experience that was especially tough. Or you might examine an experience in which you had a hard time fully believing the balanced Wise Mind view you arrived at to conclude your original debate. Or you might look for a theme within your journal entries and pick one entry to work on that's a representative sample of that core belief. If you see a theme but are still having a hard time identifying what core belief might be causing your problems, try taking the responses you've written in the "interpretations" section of a Wise Mind

Review and asking yourself the following questions:
If my worst interpretation were true in this situation . . .

". . . what would that mean about me?"
". . . what would that mean about people in general?"
". . . what would that mean about how the world works?"

(Not every question will apply in every situation, and that's okay.)

Once you have identified the core belief you think might be problematic, you are ready to complete a revised Wise Mind Debate. Following are a few specialized questions to ask yourself in a debate featuring a core belief:

"Does this belief make me feel bad?"
"How might this belief be hurting me physically in my
    relationships, my career, etc.?"
"Does this belief truly fit with my values?"
"Is this belief my own, or does it come from someone else?
    If it comes from someone else, was this person worth
    modeling in this area?"
"What evidence is there for and against my belief?"
"Who do I know that is accomplished in this area,
    and what do they believe?"
"What would I have to believe in order to feel the way
    I want to feel?"

Look for evidence to refute your core-belief thinking. Make your case. Rebut the case that the core belief is trying to keep you buying into.

Going forward, when you notice your thoughts around an emotional experience, you can ask yourself which of them may be arising from a core belief. If you think your filter may be out of date or otherwise not working for you, see if you can tell yourself a new story. Instead of "Nobody understands me," for example, you could try this on for size: "I don't have to be perfectly understood all the time" or "He's trying to understand me, but it is tough for him."

"I AM IN CHARGE OF MY THOUGHTS"

If you leave this chapter with only one thought, I want it to be this: "I am in charge of my thoughts." In very real ways, your thoughts are in charge of your emotions. You can change what you think—the interpretations you make, the story you tell yourself about what you are feeling, the worldview underpinning it all—and in doing so, you can change what you feel in order to move yourself out of Emotion Mind. It's not the only piece—what you are feeling physically and, of course, what you *do* play major parts as well. And some things you simply cannot change. But living in Wise Mind means thinking about your thinking and making it work for you.

8

CHANGE HOW YOU FEEL . . .

By Changing What You *Do*

Bonnie had been looking forward to dinner with a group of girl-friends but then got caught up with something at work at the very end of the day. When she belatedly realized the time, she rushed over to the restaurant, so hurried that she left her phone on her desk. She finally arrived, only to find that her friends had already ordered. Bonnie was livid. "What?! Are we hanging out on some kind of deadline now? They can't spare twenty minutes? Did they even notice I was missing? Obviously they didn't care! I bet it was Thea who just couldn't wait. Like she's never been late!" Bonnie stood behind the extra chair at the table, a little stunned. She felt like storming out, slamming the door behind her, and deleting all their names from her phone.

Every emotion comes with the impulse to *do* something; it's part of the cycle of emotion, following hot on the heels of your physical response and interpretation. The something you do includes not only your behavior but also your body language and facial expressions. What you say (or don't say) and how you say (or don't say) it are crucial components of what you do.

Bonnie was really, really angry—hurt—and anyone could see it by her red cheeks, her balled fists, and the look on her face. All these outward signs had happened as fast as she could list, in her mind, the indignities and unfairness of her situation. What made the difference for Bonnie that day, however, was not how she looked or felt or what she was thinking. It was what she chose to *do*, starting with choosing to file what she *wanted* to do under "not an option."

There are two important strands in a situation like Bonnie's: what you *want* to do, or feel like doing, and what you actually do, or your urge to act and your action. These actions, whether imagined or carried out, present the third and final major opportunity for changing how you feel—after changing your physical feelings and your thoughts. You may not entirely control your urge to act, as urges usually spring from that fast-moving but not exactly up-to-date dinosaur part of your brain; but you *do* control whether and how you act upon your urge. Using Wise Mind to choose your path not only helps you stay out of trouble (you might feel like screaming at the police officer who just pulled you over, but you prudently decide on deference instead) but also allows you to change the emotional experience itself. By smiling at the nice police officer and using a calm voice to inquire whether there is a problem here, officer, you make it much harder for your body and mind to get or remain overwrought. Even if you are faking that veneer of politeness. Even if you still get a ticket.

It's a good thing that you can, in fact, choose your own adventure in the face of emotion, because when your instincts are thrown into Emotion Mind, they usually drive you toward suffering more from your emotion, not less. What you really feel like doing is usually something along the lines of ruminating over what happened, trying to maintain denial, or yelling at someone you love—none of which can actually improve the situation, no matter how mightily you try. By using Wise Mind, you can choose, actively and mindfully, how to behave. You can override impulse and opt for a better course. Making a Wise Mind choice rather than an Emotion Mind choice can actually change or defuse the experience of emotion. Using Wise Mind to plot your course reduces emotional distress, even if you *can't* change either the emotion or the trigger.

Express Yourself?

Beneath every decision you make about your actions and your action urges is the essential nature of the action you take: at base, are you suppressing the emotion or expressing it? There are potential negative health consequences, physical and emotional, in both directions if you express or suppress in the wrong ways. Contrary to most people's personal preference for one way or the other, there is no "right" way to go. The path that leads to psychological health and physical wellness is emotional flexibility—that is, knowing when (and how) to express and when (and how) to suppress.

Many of us work very hard to avoid or ignore distressing emotions. But these emotions are unavoidable and will always make themselves known, one way or another. Suppressing emotion is like pushing a beach ball underwater. It takes a bit of effort, though it is possible. But eventually, that thing is going to make a break for the surface, and when it does, it will burst forth in dramatic fashion, causing much more of a stir than it did when it was just floating along on the surface, plain as day.

Your attempts to avoid or paper over emotions often lead to nothing more than a delayed bursting forth of the emotion, but bigger and "better" than ever. Suppression can also lead to a host of problems, like overeating, misuse of alcohol and drugs, financial issues, or relationship difficulties. You may think you are dealing with your emotions, but you're actually just pushing them away, distracting yourself from them in unproductive ways, or numbing yourself entirely. At best, this brings temporary relief, but it often causes more harm. (Sometimes I do recommend distracting yourself, as you'll see in the next chapter; but like anything else, you have to do it appropriately.)

Unrestrained expression doesn't work much better. You probably know people who take this kind of approach: they are overly dramatic in how they express emotion, revving themselves up and saying things like "I can't stand this" or "I can't handle it!" Whatever happened, it is the most terrible thing ever, and no one else has ever experienced such terribleness or could even hope to understand just how terrible it is: full drama-queen mode. Or there's the hair-trigger temper, going from zero to sixty in seconds in response to provocations mere mortals might not even perceive right away. And then there is expressing and expressing and expressing the same emotion without appearing to ever let go of it.

It is, of course, all about balance. Don't deny or invalidate your feeling, but don't inflate or promote it either. You need to find the middle path. Wise Mind can lead you there.

WHAT DO YOU FEEL LIKE DOING?

Each of the Big Eight emotions has its own characteristic urge to act that's just as hardwired into you as any other part of emotional reaction. Because there's a theme to what you feel like doing, depending on what your feelings are, discovering what you feel like doing (or noticing what you are in fact doing) can sometimes help you clarify which emotion you are having. (Wishing you could crawl under a rock right now? Hello, shame.) Taking note of your action urges and your actions is also useful, even if you already know "Hey, I'm really sad" before you register that what you'd very much like to do right now is get away from everyone and be left alone. Identifying your actions and desired actions is a prerequisite for being able to decide which choices are good ones. It also provides the baseline for one of the key Wise Mind Living practices: Opposite Action (page 128).

The "Urge to Act and Actions" list (page 66) provides many specific examples of urges typically associated with each of the Big Eight emotions. Reviewing the list may help you clarify your feelings and action urges. Here's a refresher on the general urges for each emotion.

Typical Action Urges

EMOTION	GENERAL URGE
Fear	Running away/avoidance
Anger	Yelling or otherwise lashing out
Sadness	Withdrawing
Shame	Hiding
Jealousy	Protecting what you have Trying to get what someone else has Tearing down someone else Trying to equalize a situation
Disgust	Getting away from/avoidance
Love	Getting closer to Getting more of Being near to
Happiness	Continuing to do what's making you happy, or doing it again, or more often Getting more of what's making you happy

Adapted from Marsha Linehan's *Skills Training Manual for Treating Borderline Personality Disorder*

Following the urge to act that comes automatically, unfiltered by Wise Mind, almost always increases the length and intensity of an emotional experience. That's all well and good when you are feeling love or happiness (within limits, as we'll see), but for distressing emotions, there's almost always a better way. Doing the first thing that pops into your head is not going to decrease the uncomfortable or painful parts of an emotional experience, no matter how appealing it seems at first to punch the wall or start hurling insults. If you feel blue and go with your first thought—to stay in bed and not talk to anyone—you will only feel worse. The more you indulge the urge, the bigger the feeling is going to get.

The one urge you do want to indulge is the one that goes something like, "Whoa, wait a minute." That urge is not always going to come to you when you are in Emotion Mind, but you can make it a habit to pause and consider before you decide to act; you can *choose* to act from Wise Mind, instead.

Mindfulness of Urges

Mindfulness, as you know, is a multipurpose tool, and this is another perfect occasion for breaking it out.

For a day or two or three, set an intention to pay attention to what your urges and actions are each time you have an emotion. Just notice them, without judgment. Don't edit yourself. Notice how you behave and what other impulses to act you have. Ask yourself: "What do I feel like doing? What do I *want* to do? What action am I taking? What am I *going* to do?"

You can write down what you notice—perhaps in a Wise Mind Review—or do the exercise during your formal meditation practice.

What Is Your Behavior Telling You?

You may find that you automatically take action as a result of an emotion, without connecting your action to that emotion. But you'll need to be able to make that connection if you want to change the emotion, the behavior, or the effects of either or both.

Many of us use behaviors to push away feelings, distract ourselves from them, or numb ourselves entirely. As a result, we often have physical- and mental-health consequences. Most of these behaviors bring temporary relief at best, but they often cause more harm: Overeating. Not eating. Sleeping too much. Not sleeping enough. Smoking more. Smoking at all! Drinking. Impulse buying.

Years ago, I worked with a Wall Street trading firm; it was my job to try to keep the traders calm and de-stressed, at least as much as that can happen amid the chaos of a trading floor. All the guys (and it was all guys) had the same pattern: when they got more emotional, they made stupid choices and "blew up" (lost money). So you can see why the firm hired me.

I asked one particular trader to keep a bare-bones diary of what he was doing day to day to see if we could find any pattern to when he was most likely to blow up. After a sleepless night? When he skipped breakfast? It didn't take long before we found some clues, though not exactly of the type we were initially looking for: it turned out that on the days he was losing money, he was smoking more cigarettes. It's not that the cigarettes were setting him up for bad trades; it was the other way around. When he was really stressing—when he was afraid he was going to blow up—he took a smoke break.

This trader wasn't registering that he was getting emotional; if you'd asked him, he wouldn't have copped to anything more than wanting a little nicotine. But he learned to recognize heading for the third cigarette of the day before 11 a.m. as a warning sign that he was in Emotion Mind and therefore wouldn't make his best trading decisions. With that knowledge, he could then decide how to act. To trade or not to trade?—that was the question. Traders trade; that's what they do. But this one learned to give himself a little time-out when the cigarettes were coming fast and furious, so he could avoid trading while in Emotion Mind.

It's not just Wall Street types who can avoid "blowing up" by being mindful of the links between their behavior and their emotions. You can do it, too, even if you don't have millions of dollars riding on how you decide to act.

WISE MIND LIVING PRACTICE
Problem Solving

Armed with what you've learned so far about your action urges and actions, you are prepared to choose your best way forward. First, decide whether any of your action urges are worth heeding. Then decide whether you should continue or cut out the actions that happened basically as reactions to a trigger. Is that scowl still what you want to keep doing? Is slumping like that conveying what you want it to convey? Are you going to keep pacing like that? Finally it's time to take a somewhat longer view: how are you going to handle whatever situation triggered this emotion? To answer this question, you're going to use Wise Mind through a process called problem solving.

Problem solving is nothing fancy or high tech. Your parents or teachers probably taught you something like it somewhere along the line. Begin by brainstorming your options and then write them down. Next, edit your list, crossing off any obvious nonstarters: things that are dangerous, things you're too chicken for, things that don't reflect your values, things that are impossible. For each item remaining on the list, ask yourself, "Would this solution cause *more* problems?" Nix any item that seems to fall into the "yes" side of that ledger. You should be down to just a few options by now, and you may be able to easily pick one. If nothing jumps out at you, do a list of pros and cons for each remaining item to choose a frontrunner.

Now try the solution. You'll get feedback from the world on how well (or how poorly) it works. Sometimes a solution seems better on paper than it does in practice. If you are not coming up with viable solutions, it may be because your emotion does not fit with the situation's objective reality. To find the right solution, you might need to back up and reconsider your interpretation. In any case, if your solution doesn't work, try another one!

OPPOSITE ACTION

Opposite action, a skill adapted from DBT, can serve as a kind of short-cut to choosing better behavior. It's very simple: whatever urge to act comes with a distressing emotion, do the exact opposite. This opposite-action practice can change even painful emotions.

Get on the plane. Go to the party. Be polite to the officer. Sit down at the table with your girlfriends, call the waiter over and place your order, and join the conversation with a smile on your face.

That last choice is the one Bonnie made. However, to manage it, she had to push thoughts of stomping away and digital erasure out of her mind. She had been working with me on using opposite action, so she knew that if she was going to stay, she had to do the thing properly. She wasn't going to sit there sulking or pick a fight right then and there. She also knew that if it didn't work, if she was still angry about the overeager ordering after the evening was over, she could always come back to the subject with her friends. She could problem-solve the best way to approach them about it. Having this Plan B in the back of her mind helped her stick with her choice to act as if she were *not* angry.

What happened instead was that after a little while, she wasn't "acting as if" anymore; she really wasn't angry. She got into the swing of the evening, enjoyed being with her friends, and found (a little bit to her surprise, if she were honest) that she simply got over it. After the heat of the moment passed, she was able to think about whether she had had a right to be *that* angry when she had been twenty minutes late and hadn't called. How long were they supposed to wait when they couldn't have known when she would arrive—or if she was even coming at all? She found she couldn't get worked up over it after all. By changing what she did—joining the party, instead of flying off the handle—Bonnie changed how she felt.

(One caveat: if the emotion you are having is fear and if you are right to feel fear because the situation is somehow actually dangerous, you should heed any action urge that keeps you safe. Caveat and a half: you may also want to carefully think through action urges from shame before outing yourself about something so you can protect yourself if that something actually will get you rejected.)

Opposite Actions

EMOTION	OPPOSITE ACTIONS
Fear	Do what you are afraid of doing (only if the fear is unjustified). Do not avoid what you fear (only if the fear is unjustified). Do something that makes you feel in control. Make a list of small steps toward your goal and do the first thing on the list.
Anger	"Gently avoid" the person you are angry at (rather than attacking or giving him or her the cold shoulder). Avoid thinking about the person you are angry with (rather than ruminating). Do something nice (rather than something mean or attacking). Imagine sympathy and empathy for the other person (rather than blame).
Sadness	Socialize. Call a friend. Get active. Do not avoid what's making you sad. Do something that makes you feel competent and self-confident.
Shame	Do what makes you feel guilt or shame (as long as it doesn't actually go against your values). Tell someone what you are ashamed of. (Choose the person carefully.) Apologize. Make amends. Repair damage. Do something nice for the person you offended (or for someone else if that's not possible). Commit to not repeating the behavior. Accept consequences gracefully. Let it go.
Jealousy	Stop spying or snooping. Let go of your attempts at controlling or limiting others' actions. Share what you have. Make a list of what you are thankful for.
Disgust	Don't avoid the food, item, or person you found disgusting. Be kind to the person you dislike.

Adapted from Marsha Linehan's *Skills Training Manual for Treating Borderline Personality Disorder*

"I DON'T WANT TO ACT OPPOSITE—
I'M FEELING HAPPY!"

You might have noticed that there are no opposite actions included for love and happiness. In general, the more love and happiness you have, the better, so I'm not going to tell you to go around reining in those emotions by acting as if you were *not* happy.

Except for the exceptions, of course—even happiness needs curbing sometimes. The action urge for happiness is to do more of whatever is making you happy. Imagine, though, that eating this nice piece of chocolate cake is making you feel happy. Doing more and more of that—consuming piece after piece of chocolate cake—is eventually going to make you very *un*happy. So you want your pursuit of happiness to stay on the sensory-pleasure side of the line, without crossing over into indigestion or obesity territory.

With happiness and love, the two things to watch out for are these: constantly chasing positive emotions (by doing so, you just set yourself up for disappointment; besides, if you are always running, you never arrive) and getting carried away by good feelings. Happiness and love are forms of Emotion Mind, too, after all. You don't want to let them take precedence over logical, reasonable choices any more than you want fear or anger to take over. You want Wise Mind in charge of positive emotions, not just distressing ones. If you go shopping in happiness Emotion Mind (say, you just got a big bonus check), then you're liable to end up buying something lovely that you simply can't afford. Next weekend, when the initial thrill of holding that check in your hand has subsided (so you are not in Emotion Mind anymore), you can make a better decision about whether this item is in fact the way you want to draw down your bank account balance.

Love's action urges come with a particular brand of potential problems that you want to steer clear of: if you love and that love is not returned, for example, opposite action is just the thing. It beats writing an unrequited love's name over and over on the cover of your algebra notebook! Or consider what happens when love for your kids or partner or parents drives you to sacrifice yourself to the point at which you never say no and aren't getting what you need. Pouring so much focus into retaining the positive feeling of love that you neglect your own self is not Wise!

Body Language

The path between emotion and body language runs two ways. An emotion comes with a tendency toward certain postures, expressions, and gestures, like slumping when you're sad or shaking a fist when you're angry. But that same body language reinforces the experience of the emotion. If you put on, or hold on to, the body language, you will keep feeling the emotion. What you do with your body signals the brain. Cower, and the signal is to feel afraid. Smile, and the signal is to feel happy. Release the clenched hands or the scowl or the turned-away face, and you signal the brain to let go of the whole emotion.

As automatic as it can seem, body language is an action or behavior—a really important one, because of how strongly it affects how we are perceived, but a behavior nonetheless. No matter what I tell someone else about how I feel, if I am displaying emotion with my body, the other person will believe what my body is saying over what's coming out of my mouth. Every time.

Adopting your desired body language (not the one affected more or less automatically by the emotion) can be the most important way you act opposite. It's critical to the success of any other opposite action you might attempt; if it doesn't match your body language, it is going to fail. The change in your body might even be all you need to change the emotion.

WISE MIND LIVING PRACTICE
Opposite Action

The only instruction you really need to put Opposite Action into practice is this: go all out. Whatever you determine to be the opposite action you are going to take, you have to do it 100 percent. Your body language and your facial expression have to be on board. You have to look the part. You have to be invested. You have to do your best. You have to be a good actor!

Imagine if Bonnie had taken the opposite action of sitting down to dinner rather than leaving the restaurant in a huff, but then sat at the table looking daggers at Thea, the imagined instigator of premature ordering, or even just refusing to contribute to the chatter around her. This is not a convincing display of *not* being angry. Her friends wouldn't be fooled, and neither would she. Her emotion, and the distress she felt from it, wouldn't budge.

When you are doing Opposite Action, especially as a beginner, it's a good idea to record the way in which you acted opposite: the emotion, what you wanted to do, and what you did do. You can do this in a separate Wise Mind Living journal entry, though it fits right into the Wise Mind Review exercise (page 47).

LIVING IN WISE MIND
Brad Acts Opposite

For my patient Brad, acting opposite—body language and all—was the key to breaking out of the grip of severe social anxiety. A lot of people feel a bit nervous when meeting new people or navigating a crowd. But for Brad, the feelings were so intense, he spent his evenings and weekends at home alone. This wasn't exactly what he had envisioned for himself when he moved out of his hometown to the big city. His new coworkers invited him to do things, and so did the handful of his old friends who had made the move before him. But no matter what the offer was or who made it, Brad never went. He came to me for help because, he said, he felt lonely and depressed. He *wanted* to go out for drinks after work or catch a ball game, but he just couldn't do it.

The first step for Brad was to realize that loneliness and sadness were secondary emotions and that he needed to focus on the primary emotion—fear—that was keeping him at home and creating that loneliness and sadness. He agreed that if he were able to go out with friends, connect with people (maybe even new people), and have a good time—if he could find a way to defeat the worries that kept him from socializing—he would likely be rid of the sadness and the loneliness.

This is a job for Acting Opposite Man! With social anxiety, the more you expose yourself to what you fear—that is, the more you actually do socialize—the less the force of the emotion. For Brad, what constituted Acting Opposite was clear: When his inclination was to just go home, he had to go out. While he was used to saying, "No, thanks," he now had to accept invitations. (In fact, he had to get to the place where he could *issue* the invitations.) And he needed to *talk* to people when he went out—look them in the eye and talk.

I ran down the most important rule of the game for Brad, the one about committing to his opposite action 100 percent. Going to a party and not talking to a soul did not count. He could go with a friend for support, but he had to engage in conversation with other people, fully throwing himself in. No fair talking only to that friend, schlumping alongside him looking unapproachable, or sitting like a bump on a log. Brad had to be all-in.

I advised him to select his social events carefully: no sense choosing a party where he doesn't know anyone or some other "worst case" scenario.

We also brainstormed some small ways Brad could start this process so he could build up to a full-fledged outing with some positive experiences already under his belt. He decided to try smiling at one new person (at least) every day, whether in passing on the street, in the grocery store, or wherever the day took him. The first week, he giddily reported that almost everyone *smiled back*. Using this incremental approach, Brad saw no sign of what he feared: no one was mean, and there was no evidence of people not liking him or not thinking highly of him. The same thing happened the following week, when Brad joined the regular Wednesday happy hour with his colleagues. Everyone seemed as pleasant as they did in the office—a little more so, actually, after the first pitcher of beer. In fact, he found it easier to chat with people at work after he'd spent some social time with them, which, to his surprise, turned down his work stress a notch.

After a few weeks, Brad decided he was ready to try a bigger hurdle and went to a cookout one of his buddies was throwing at the park.

He went with another friend and knew there would be a few other familiar faces there—but there were a lot of new people, too. Brad brought his Frisbee, thinking he might be able to get up a game, and that turned out to be a good way to connect in an easy way with people he didn't know—giving people a reason to come up to him, giving him a reason to approach other people, and providing them all with some starter chitchat.

When one of those new acquaintances mentioned a pickup basketball game the next weekend, Brad said he'd like to join. And he knew he would. It took several more social occasions before Brad really left behind the worst of his anxiety for good—fortified by tips and tricks he'd learned to make socializing easier and an array of strategies for handling any anxiety that did arise—but he could see he was going to get there. As he added events to his calendar, Brad quickly stopped feeling lonely. And as he gained confidence that attending these events did not result in rejection, his feelings of sadness abated as well. And all of that, in the end, made it a little easier for him to be social.

Brad had to ignore almost all of his initial action urges: they were urging him to go home and stay home. When he used Wise Mind to choose more effective actions, he not only changed the results of his behavior, but he also changed the emotion providing those unhelpful action urges. He changed how he felt by changing what he did. ⦾

WISE MIND ACTION

When you choose which action urges to heed, when you change what you do in the grip of emotion, you move away from Emotion Mind and toward Wise Mind. Wise Mind Living means responding thoughtfully to emotion rather than reacting habitually. And that's what allows you to find your best course of action.

9

WHEN YOU CAN'T CHANGE HOW YOU FEEL

Acceptance and Coping

So, we've been talking about the fact that you are in charge of your emotions. If you don't like the way you feel, you have lots of options for how to go about changing that. We've also discussed how managing your emotions is the key to health and happiness.

But, of course, sometimes stuff happens that you don't control. Sometimes you can't change whatever is triggering a distressing emotion. Sometimes you feel really, really lousy, and there's not a thing you can do about it.

Sometimes you can't change your circumstances, and you are pretty much stuck with the distressing emotions those circumstances are triggering. Sometimes you can't change your emotion . . . *yet:* you are too worked up, too much in Emotion Mind, and not quite in touch with how to be different. When you can't change how you feel (or *while* you can't change how you feel), you can still use Wise Mind Living strategies to change how you cope with how you are feeling.

You should definitely change distressing emotions when you can. But sometimes you can't, so you also need to learn to accept and cope with distressing emotions when that's the only way forward. The goal is to get through the moment without doing something negative and without thinking or acting in ways that make things worse or that create (or increase) suffering. Then do it again to get through the next moment. And the next.

To move through moments like these, you need both specific skills (coping) and a more general attitude (acceptance). You may need to pursue another activity to distract or soothe yourself, setting aside the emotion for a while, even if you don't get rid of it. You may simply need to let time pass—and the intensity of emotion to lessen as it does. Then you may find that you can effectively manage what remains. Or you may need to just feel the feeling and experience getting through it. You can make an active choice to take the edge off your painful emotions while you are in the midst of them, when you can't change them, or until you are ready to change them.

"DAMN THIS TRAFFIC JAM"

When I teach these skills to my patients, I often use the example of being stuck in terrible traffic on your way to an important meeting. This causes distressing emotions! Yet you can do nothing about the oversupply of cars (undersupply of highway?). So what do you do? Here are some options:

1. *Fuss and fume.* Be sure to clench your teeth, curse, and perhaps grumble about the driver in front of you not moving up promptly when the car ahead of *him* creeps forward. Save some choice words for the person who set the meeting for a time when you'd have to fight through rush hour. And your spouse, who just *had* to have that conversation this morning that got you out of the house five minutes late. Also the department of transportation, or whoever designed these merge lanes, because they are *not* working efficiently.

2. *Fiddle with the radio until you get a good song and sing along at the top of your lungs.* Or tune in to that program you love but never get a chance to hear all of. Or, you know that thing you've been meaning to get to? Now's your chance to really think it through.

3. *Focus on how late you are.* Keep checking your watch. Think about all the trouble you're in now. Dwell on how you should have set the alarm earlier and taken that other route. Remember: you are late, late, *late!*

4. *Take a few slow breaths.* Acknowledge to yourself that you are going to miss this meeting. Acknowledge that you are just going to have to sit here for a while. Yep, it feels lousy. Don't even pretend you are happy about it. It's a sucky situation; that's all there is to it.

So, which one do you do?

Trick question! Because there are two right answers: either #2 or #4 can get you through while minimizing your misery. You can't avoid the traffic once you're stuck in it, and missing the meeting is going to cause distressing emotions, no doubt about it. But finding a way to cope with those feelings and accept the situation for what it is allows you to lessen its negative impact on you.

Buddhists talk about this as the difference between pain and suffering. Everyone experiences pain, in doses small ("Argh! We finally got a date night, and now the movie is sold out!") and large (divorce). Pain is a part of life, no matter what. Suffering, on the other hand, is optional. Suffering is the result of how we handle our pain. You can't get a pass on pain, but you do *not* have to have suffering; in fact, how much you suffer is up to you. In the example of being trapped in a snarl of traffic, you create your own suffering when you deal with the pain (the traffic) by ruminating about it, finding others to blame, and generally underlining to yourself how terrible it is and how overwhelmed you are by it.

Grace to accept with serenity the things that cannot be changed,
Courage to change the things which should be changed,
And the Wisdom to distinguish the one from the other.
REINHOLD NEIBUHR

ACCEPTANCE

Suffering is essentially the opposite of acceptance. If you are suffering, you are not accepting; if you are not accepting, you are going to suffer. Want to not suffer? Practice acceptance.

Acceptance is an attitude, a state of mind, a perspective. Okay, so it's a pretty abstract concept, a bit hard to describe, and I can't tell you exactly how it is done: there's no list of exact step-by-step instructions—which is too bad, because it's an absolute touchstone of emotional regulation, despite the lack of a clearly blazed trail. You simply have to *do* it. Try it. Experience it. Practice it. Cultivate it. Say to yourself, "It is what it is, and I can't change it right now." Recognize the situation, acknowledge your emotions—especially the ones that are making you feel crummy—and just allow it all to *be*. Choose answer #4.

Acceptance is *not* ignoring or stuffing an emotion or burying your head in the sand. It is not being a doormat or an easy mark. Acceptance does not mean giving up the attempt to change the way things are. Acceptance is perspective (not passivity). It is making a choice (not leaving things to chance). It is putting an emotion away on the shelf for a while, where you can keep an eye on it. You can reach it if you need it, but it is out of the way for now.

Here is the thing about acceptance: choosing to accept things as they are, relinquishing the struggle that leads to suffering, is actually the path to change. It's the path to more effective, mindful change—change that is responsive rather than reactive. Without acceptance, you can get stuck in the cycle of emotion, unable to find the off-ramp and unable to figure out how or what you might be able to change. There will always be some circumstantial facts you can never change, but the true transformation comes about within yourself.

WISE MIND LIVING PRACTICE
Catch Yourself in Nonacceptance

For at least a day or two or three, be on the lookout for the little moments of nonacceptance you have throughout the day. While you're at it, you may as well check for any big things in life that you are not really accepting. Big or small, just notice anything that you keep wishing were different—even if, when you stop to think about it, you would say it is not likely to change any time soon. Are you irked by the broiling temperature—in July? Provoked by that nosy neighbor? Think you are underpaid? See if there's a refrain in your head that sounds something like, "I can't take this," "How could this happen?!?" "I *hate* this," or the classic, "This should be different." That's a clue that you are struggling against something rather than accepting it. If your best friend would tell you that you are in denial about something—well, that's a form of nonacceptance, too.

Here's how I caught myself recently. I was on my way to pick up my son, a bit behind schedule, and waiting for an elevator. And waiting. And waiting. I pushed the call button over and over and over again, and the elevator *still* did not arrive any faster! So now I had two problems: a little anxiety that I'd be late to retrieve my son from his very first day at a new camp *and* a failure to understand how elevators work. Three problems, actually, because I was in active nonacceptance, struggling against the plain fact that I was simply going to have to wait for the elevator to arrive before I could be on my way. I was really mad at that elevator!

Until it dawned on me what I was doing. I took a couple slow breaths, unclenched my jaw, and then laughed at myself and my button pushing. And just like that, I moved to acceptance. I was going to be late for the pickup; that was what it was, and I couldn't change it. I could stop stressing myself even more by no longer mashing my finger into the elevator button and pacing and sighing like a condemned woman. I reminded myself that my son was well cared for and that he would still be at camp whenever I arrived. I couldn't change the circumstances or the emotion that the situation generated, but I could change how I handled both—and that's what made all the difference.

WISE MIND LIVING PRACTICE
Be Kind to Yourself

In the midst of a difficult emotional experience, take a moment to acknowledge your suffering. Being compassionate toward yourself can be quite soothing.

Sit comfortably and breathe to center yourself. When you are ready, slowly repeat to yourself several times, "I am in pain, but I can handle this." Staying connected to your breath, tell yourself, "Let me be kind to myself." Actually, you can fill in your own blank after "Let me . . ." with whatever comforts you.

Here are some suggestions:

Let me . . .
". . . feel safe."
". . . find peace."
". . . accept myself and my life."
". . . let go of this suffering."
". . . know I can take care of myself."
". . . remember there will come a time when I will feel better."

Or use one of the coping statements (page 143). Whatever words you choose, the underlying message that you deliver to yourself, that you want yourself to really believe, is that you can tolerate and handle it—whatever "it" is. You are strong enough. You can allow the feelings. And this, too, shall pass.

Acknowledge and show compassion toward yourself and your situation and your emotions.

You can do this exercise while emotions are stirred up. But you can also do it while reflecting on something upsetting that has happened (but isn't happening right at this very moment). Call to mind what you want to work on and give yourself compassion around it. This will work best on things that distress you, but are not *so* distressing that you can't think straight. In ultra-distressing situations, you may need to do some other exercises before you are ready for a self-compassion break.

Be Forgiving

Forgiveness is closely related to acceptance and is yet another topic to which entire books have been devoted. What you need to know about forgiveness to make Wise Mind Living work for you is that to reach acceptance, you often need to forgive first. Forgive yourself. Forgive the person you feel caused the painful feelings in you. Make the choice to turn your mind to another way of thinking. Without forgiveness, you will not be able to move on, and you will be stuck short of reaching acceptance.

Take my patient who failed to pay his taxes one year. It's a long story, but the gist of it is that several years have gone by since he didn't pay. He's now married, running a successful business, paying all his taxes—and facing a bill for back taxes from that year. He's also facing a pissed-off spouse, who is not really any madder at my patient than he is at himself. If they are going to get past this, she is going to have to forgive him. But he is also going to have to forgive himself. This thing happened, and there's nothing he can do to change that fact now. He must learn from it (and, in fact, he demonstrably has), and he must move past it. And he can only accomplish that through forgiveness.

 WISE MIND LIVING PRACTICE
Observer Mind-Set and Teflon Mind

Cultivating an observer mind-set is the foundation of mindfulness practice. The idea is to tune in to your experience exactly as it is, observing without judging and without pushing anything away *or* clutching on to any of it. See? Mindfulness. It becomes an acceptance practice when you take it out and drive it around in the middle of distressing circumstances that you can't change.

When something is annoying, upsetting, irritating, or devastating, step back a little and simply observe your experience as if you were viewing it from the outside, as if you were not at the beating heart of it. You want to be slightly detached but still clearly an interested party. Some of my patients say they imagine they are news reporters, gathering all the facts and relaying what's most important about what happened, but never getting sucked into the middle of the "story." With this approach, even when there is pain, you don't create suffering.

"Teflon mind" takes this practice one step further. You assume the observer mind-set, observe your experience, and then set the intention to not let anything distressing stick to you. Whatever it is that bothers you—or would if it could stick, which it can't, because you are like Teflon—let it slide right off. Include that information in your report to yourself. When someone pushes your buttons, observe to yourself, "That person is really pushing my buttons, but I'm going to let it all bounce right off me." And move on.

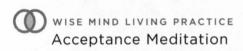 WISE MIND LIVING PRACTICE
Acceptance Meditation

This is a simple way to practice acceptance on the spot. Take a slow breath (a cleansing breath, as my yoga teacher says), try to relax the tension in your body, and adopt an "open" posture: shoulders back, chin up, spine straight. Now breathe slowly, fully, and evenly, and say to yourself as you breathe in, "Everything is," and, as you breathe out, "as it should be." Or use (inhaling) "It is" (exhaling) "what it is." As you breathe, see if you can relax and open your body and your mind to the idea that you believe exactly what you are saying.

HEALTHY COPING

Wise Mind Living provides two paths through the briar patch of Things You Can't Change. Acceptance is one of them. But there is another, more concrete way as well: coping skills. In DBT, it's called "distress tolerance," since the main point is to tolerate distressing emotions. You're in this situation, you have these feelings, and they're sticking around: how best to bear up? If you can't change the moment, your best bet is to get through it with as little negative impact on you as possible. This is not always easy to accomplish in the heat of the moment, but there are a few straightforward skills you can learn to call on as needed.

Distraction

Give your brain something else to do besides rehashing your distressing emotion and railing against the unchangeable circumstances that brought it forth. Do something that engages your brain so it's too busy with this something else to fret. (Try to recall a whole song, not just the chorus; see if you can name all the U.S. presidents or put the fifty states in alphabetical order; solve for *x* in your head.) Do something, anything, rather than just sitting there stewing. (Go for a run, call a friend, or start a new project around the house.) Create a more intense physical sensation than the one that comes with the emotion you're having—perhaps by taking a very hot bath or really pushing yourself in a workout or splashing cold water on your face or holding an ice cube in your hand. Your brain needs a different task, and you're going to provide it.

An excellent form of distraction is to do something for someone else, something that contributes something to the world. It shifts your focus away from your pain and creates positive meaning in your life to counterbalance the negative.

Inaction

On the other hand, you could do nothing. Actually, you can do this at the same time you are working on distraction. Or distraction can help you achieve inaction. In this game, if you do *not* act on the negative urges that come with a distressing emotion, you win. Another way to practice this same skill is to just let time pass. (The "It Gets Better" Internet campaign is not only a long-term version of this but also a good summary of the idea behind the inaction strategy.) Either way you conceive of it, if you are not doing anything to make matters worse, you are coping with distress. You are also making room to try things that will take the edge off, helping you get through the moment.

Self-Soothing

Be good to yourself. Do something that makes you feel comforted, relaxed, and cared for. Get a hug, take a nap, soak in the tub, listen to your favorite CD, watch trashy TV, do a guided meditation, or pray, if that appeals to you. I gave this assignment to one overwrought client at the end of a session, and her immediate response was, "I'm taking a cab home." She knew what would make her life a little easier that day, what would give her that little extra breathing room she needed.

And good for her, too, because a lot of us are pretty lousy at knowing what soothes us! So *your* assignment is to brainstorm a list for yourself, so that you don't have to suddenly come up with something right when you urgently need it. Those of you most clueless in this area might have to try out a bunch of things and then decide what works for you and put those on the list. Or you might have to think about what you would do for others—if someone you loved were in need of soothing. Or think back to what you *used* to find soothing—things you've done in the past but drifted away from. Maybe you used to plink away at the piano or knit or sit in the sun—and maybe you'd still enjoy those things if you allowed yourself time for them.

Once you have your list, make sure you have on hand anything that might be required to do these pleasant activities. Stock up on a supply of bubble bath or *People* magazines or relaxation CDs or whatever. You want to be ready to go when the need arises. You should also consider incorporating these strategies into your life, even when you don't *need* them: sort of like a preventative measure of stress release.

One caveat comes with these coping strategies: it's possible—not even very hard, actually—to go overboard with the distraction and self-soothing. So please note: moderation, people! I'm talking about using these techniques in sensible doses, as needed, not about ignoring problems, giving up, or stuffing emotions. You want to get a brief break from life, not avoid life altogether.

Coping Statements

Whether you are dealing with unhelpful thoughts or problematic core beliefs, one simple way to switch to a more productive way of thinking is to use coping statements. The idea is to give your thoughts a better track to run along. Try reminding yourself that whatever is going on, whatever has upset you, you *can* cope. You have to. You will.

People are much better at helping other people feel better than they are at helping themselves. If you stop to notice it, your inner dialogue is pretty negative when you are feeling down. You may tell yourself things you would *never* say to a friend or loved one in pain. To them, you'd offer validation ("I totally understand how you feel"), reassurance ("You can handle this"), and perspective ("It won't feel this bad forever"). What if you could be as supportive toward yourself?

While you are waiting for the worst to pass, try talking to yourself more wisely with coping statements like these:

> "I'm strong enough to handle what's happening
>   right now."
> "It's okay to feel crappy sometimes."
> "This too shall pass."
> "These feelings aren't dangerous; they're just
>   uncomfortable."
> "My feelings are making me uncomfortable right
>   now, but I can accept them."
> "I can ride this out and not let it get to me."
> "I can think about this differently if I want to."
> "I can feel bad and still deal with the situation effectively."
> "I'm going to take really good care of myself while I
>   am feeling this bad."
> "I am going to just take it moment by moment."
> "Okay, so it isn't how I would like it to be. So what?"
> "This is an opportunity for me to practice all the
>   skills I have been learning to master my emotions."

WISE MIND LIVING PRACTICE
Thought Diffusion

In Emotion Mind, you tend to get stuck in your thoughts. Thought diffusion is the Wise Mind Living way to sweep out whatever is buzzing around unhelpfully in your head. It's a sort of visual mindfulness meditation, and it has many variations. Try them all, pick your favorite, or make up your own.

- Imagine your thoughts are like clouds in the sky, and let them drift by above you.
- Visualize a stream, and let each thought be a leaf floating on it. Watch them all float downstream, sailing out of sight.
- Picture yourself driving down a highway, and let each of the billboards along the road contain one of your thoughts. The thoughts stay right where they are; you whiz by, leaving them behind.

In each case, your challenge is to *not* follow the train of thought or the path of your thinking. The theme of the visualizations, you probably noticed, is of those thoughts getting farther away from where you are. They are not attached to you; your job is to remain unattached to them.

You can use this technique at any time to practice mindfulness. Your thoughts don't necessarily have to relate to distressing emotions; they can be any thoughts that are taking you away from being in the here and now. It is also great to do this right before you go to sleep or when you are having trouble getting to sleep. You can use Thought Diffusion when you know you are in Emotion Mind, when the thinking you are doing is not going to get you anyplace good. Try it when you need to calm your body and brain enough for you to move on to change strategies. Perhaps most of all, though, Thought Diffusion is an excellent choice when you are facing down a situation and distressing emotions that you can't change.

What does *not* work, however, is thought *stopping*. You cannot just make your thoughts not come to you or disappear altogether.

> We don't receive wisdom; we must discover it for ourselves
> after a journey that no one can take for us or spare us.
>
> MARCEL PROUST

SIT WITH YOUR EMOTION

When I suggest to my patients that they just sit there and feel their emotions—the good, the bad, and the ugly—many eagerly point out that I am contradicting myself. Wasn't I just talking about putting emotion on a shelf, distracting, letting stuff float downstream without even trying to grab it back? Many of them look at me as if I must be off my rocker, because haven't they just been saying how fervently they would like to *not* feel these painful emotions?

I know just what they mean about that last bit. Several years ago, my father had a recurrence of cancer and, for lack of other options, started on what was then an experimental chemo regimen. Somewhere in the middle of this whirlwind, I stopped meditating. I didn't really choose to do that or even really notice it. I was just so busy and preoccupied with worry that my meditation practice sort of fell away. Once I realized what was going on, I gave myself my own advice: "*This* is the reason you meditate—so that you will be ready to take this kind of thing on. Sit down and feel your feelings."

But I really, really didn't want to. Wasn't I struggling enough as it was? Wasn't I feeling plenty of grief, sadness, fear, the works? At least a month went by this way, and a miserable month it was. The very last thing I wanted to do was stop and pay attention to my suffering.

Eventually, though, I did just that, thanks to a meditation retreat I had scheduled long before my father's health crisis started. I had to force myself to attend and force myself to do even the most basic mindfulness meditation. When I finally did, I experienced the healing power of doing so. Of course, I had not escaped any of my painful feelings by avoiding meditation. Worse, I hadn't really given myself credit for all I *was* in fact feeling, try as I might to avoid approaching it face on. When I finally sat down to feel it all, mindfully, I actually felt *less* anxious. Here I was, feeling it and surviving; maybe I didn't have to work so frantically to keep the feelings at bay. I learned that I could handle it—that I *was* handling it. This is the same key insight so many of my patients gain from sitting with their emotions. Pouring so many resources into maintaining avoidance to keep from feeling things in a big way, as I had been, meant fewer resources for handling the real issues. Better to sit and feel the emotions, work with them, metabolize them. It let me cultivate a calmness around dealing with my father's diagnosis. It couldn't take the pain away, but I was able to begin tolerating it and accepting the situation for what it was.

So I'll say to you what I say to my patients and what I said to myself: just try it. You don't have to sit for hours. You can sit for just five minutes, if you want. You can go do something soothing afterward to make yourself feel better. But if you want to experience how paying attention to what you are feeling helps you feel less of it, you just have to try it.

 WISE MIND LIVING PRACTICE
Mindfulness of Emotion

There's no real list of instructions for how to sit with your emotion. It's really just a matter of applying mindfulness to a current state of distressing emotion. Shine a light on the feeling; make it your focus.

Breathe with your emotion. Aim to be open to the moment, to yourself, and to the distress. Acknowledge that you are in the midst of painful emotion. Allow yourself to experience the emotion. Don't judge the emotion or yourself for having it—or however you've handled it thus far. Have compassion for yourself. Strive to get some perspective. Remember that you are not your emotion. Remember that there have been times when you did not feel like this. Intend to let time go by, and know that doing so will lessen the intensity of your emotion.

Remember: paying attention to what you are feeling helps you feel less of it. Mindfulness can help you let go of painful emotions so that you won't suffer from them. Sometimes that is enough.

LIVING IN WISE MIND
How Jesse Found a New Job by Just Sitting There

My friend Jesse discovered the power of sitting with painful emotions after he was laid off from a job he'd loved and had been very good at. But he did not discover this right away, of course. The pain of the job loss was followed by the pain of the job search. Despite his plan to treat finding a new position as a full-time job, it soon seemed like playing online Boggle was a nine-to-five gig. Every morning he'd fire up his laptop as soon as the kids got off to school—and start playing games. Oh, he might make a call or two, send off some emails, but there always came a point when he'd get "stuck." Like he'd hit a brick wall and didn't know what to do next, as he described it. Or he *knew* what to do next but didn't know how to go about it. So he'd take a "break," often in the form of online games. He soon racked up high scores on a quite a variety of them. He hadn't scored so many job leads or interviews, though. The "breaks" were many and extended.

Jesse explained all this one day over dinner. I asked him what he thought he was afraid of. On this social occasion, I wasn't wearing my therapist hat; apparently I had jumped ahead of him in the process a bit, because he just looked at me and said, "What do you mean, 'afraid of'?"

I hadn't actually asked him—and he'd never asked himself—what he was feeling in those moments when he decided to give up on the task at hand and play a few rounds of Boggle instead. He had been focusing on the games themselves as the source of the problem. Like so many of my patients—like so many people in general—Jesse was barking up the wrong tree. The key to solving his problem was to realize that he was feeling an emotion, identify *which* emotion, learn to experience the emotion in full, and then accept it.

As we talked about it more, Jesse pinpointed what was going through his head when he got "stuck": "You suck at this. In fact, you just suck. No wonder you can't find a job. You're never going to find another job. Even if you do, it's never going to be as good as the last one." He could see, of course, that these thoughts were not exactly helping him in his search. He thought maybe the games had such a grip on him because he was good at those, and he had the top scores to prove it. I explained a little about mindfulness practices; I recommended he try just sitting still and tuning in to what he was feeling each time he hit the wall and was ready to give in to the games. He looked skeptical but said he might give it a try.

A few days later, Jesse called to say he had taken time out to consider what he was feeling; what it all boiled down to was fear. He was afraid of not having a job, of not finding a job, and of what would happen to his family and his home if he didn't start making some money again soon. (And, as he figured out somewhat further along in the process, he was afraid of not knowing who he even *was* without a job to describe a large part of his identity.)

But he was still playing a lot of games. And he was a bit ticked with me, because as it turns out, he really didn't like feeling fear.

I suggested that he was ready for a shift in his practice. Now that he'd found out about the fear, I recommended he try sitting with it to feel it fully, the full weight and force of it. Spend some time really feeling afraid.

Allowing yourself to feel really bad is nobody's idea of a good time, and I couldn't even offer him a really good explanation for how and why it would help. It's not something that's been pinned down in a lab somewhere (at least not yet). But it's an experiential way to learn about the emotion and your ability to feel and survive it. Actually experiencing the emotion provides a kind of freedom from it. It can no longer imprison you the same way it does when you are trying so hard to get rid of it or ignore it or hide it (by, say, zoning out with a game). There's less anxiety layered on top of whatever your primary emotion is; there's no longer a need to worry about feeling it when you have already done that.

Having come this far, Jesse decided he might as well give sitting with his emotions a try. After a few times of sitting there, feeling really lousy, he had the same kind of transformational experience I've heard many patients report. He felt the fear—and then he just kept going. It didn't make the fear go away, but it made a kind of crack in it, weakening its hold on him so he could go on with what he needed to do to pursue a new job. Three days later, he had not one but two interviews lined up—and not coincidentally, only about that same number of game-playing "breaks" each day.

The kind of enlightenment that comes from allowing yourself to really feel your emotions can be short-lived, however. It's a lesson you have to keep teaching yourself. Jesse went on to get stuck more than once as his job search continued, but he was always able to get himself unstuck. Even in his new job, he still got stuck sometimes, but he knew he had a tool he could reach for any time he hit a block. With experience, he developed a shortcut: he found he could say to himself, "There I go again. I always get these self-doubts from fear, and I start to think I can't do it." Then he could choose to push through. Jesse knew there'd be times when he felt fear, but now he knew how to work through those times without getting in his own way. He'd put the final piece—acceptance—in place on his own. ⚭

ACCEPTANCE IS A MOMENT-TO-MOMENT PROPOSITION

You have to keep choosing acceptance. It is a choice to switch to a new track. You choose it in the moment you are in . . . and then, in the next moment, you must choose again. There is no long-term parking lot at acceptance.

I experienced this quite literally when I got a tattoo (of a mantra that's particularly meaningful to me, for the record). I brought a friend with me for moral support, and fortunately, I chose a friend who meditates. About two seconds into the whole thing, I was really getting the full experience of how painful getting a tattoo can be, and I could barely think about anything else. My friend encouraged me to breathe into it and to do an acceptance meditation. It took her a minute to get through to me and for me to manage it, but soon I was in a groove with (inhaling) "Just this moment" (exhaling) "I am here" (inhaling) "Everything is" (exhaling) "as it should be," speaking calmly to myself like a champ. "Just this moment, I am here. Everything is as it should be. Just this moment, I am here. . . ." I knew I could handle it, the pain subsided, and I began to congratulate myself: "Hey! This is really working!" Just like that, it began to hurt like hell again—literally the very moment I stopped practicing acceptance. If I wanted the whole tattoo and not a partial phrase, I was going to have to choose acceptance. Again.

So I did. I turned my mind back to the acceptance mantra, returned to focusing on my breath. It wasn't the last time I had to do that either. But each time I did, I stopped struggling against the situation ("Ow! This hurts! I want this to stop!") and therefore stopped the suffering. My inner mantra saw me through to the completion of my inky one.

THE RIGHT TOOLS FOR THE JOB

Wise Mind Living is all about combining the tools of change with the tools of acceptance. The trick is to know when to use which tool and which jobs require items from both toolboxes. In general, you change what you can and accept/cope with what you can't change. Often you'll use coping strategies or acceptance to get you through until you are able to work on change. Life usually requires that you mix it up a bit. You might work on changing your physiology first, then use distraction to cope with what you are feeling, then accept that you are going to feel this way for a little while, and then come around to trying to change your emotion or your circumstance.

The exact combination and order may vary, and that's fine—as long as you (1) acknowledge how you are feeling (no stuffing or ignoring) and (2) choose and apply your tools mindfully. That's how you "live" Wise Mind. In a nutshell: be mindful of what you are feeling and then set and hold an intention for what you are doing and how and why you are doing it.

10

SIX WEEKS TO
WISE MIND LIVING

This is where Wise Mind meets Living. Most people learn how to access Wise Mind in two phases. You've just finished phase one—reading the first nine chapters of this book, learning the principles of Wise Mind, and beginning to practice some of the exercises. With this chapter, you are beginning phase two, shifting from learning Wise Mind to living it. You're still learning, of course, but this section is about getting it off the page and into practical usage.

Wise Mind is a state that gets easier to reach and maintain with practice. It is also something you never stop practicing—you can't just get to Wise Mind and stay there. It's more like the place you're always aiming for, so you can always be on the right path en route. It's the journey, not the destination. Among other things, this means you may find yourself going back through the book again, even after you finish the program in this chapter. In fact, for most of my patients, two times through both phases (learn, live, learn more, live more fully) is usual before they feel Wise Mind Living is really *theirs*.

This chapter offers a six-week program, because six weeks is enough time to give you a powerful experience of what Wise Mind Living is like and what its benefits are. But you don't just do six weeks and then sit back to admire your completed project. You need to play on.

You don't have to wait six weeks to benefit from Wise Mind Living strategies, though. Most of my patients experience at least some relief from the very first week they begin some of these practices. Whether or not you master everything in all six weeks on the first go, the bottom line is this: *you are about to feel better.*

Wise Mind Living is a continual balancing act between acceptance and change. You will find that the first half of this six-week program focuses more on awareness and acceptance, and the second half, on change. In real life, you need to move along a continuum between these polarities with a certain amount of flexibility. Change what you can and accept what you can't. Part of what you'll learn is how to know the difference!

We're going to take this step by step. Each week of this program, you will focus on practicing a particular skill (a skill you will carry forward into the following weeks). Each week also has suggested daily mindfulness practices, Wise Mind Living journal "homework" assignments, and a reminder about which chapters cover related material. You'll keep going with practices you've begun while reading through the first nine chapters (and if you haven't begun them yet, what are you waiting for?), and you'll add a few new ones. In this way, week by week, you will accumulate all you need to fill your Wise Mind Living toolbox.

Anyone can do this. But it does require real work and commitment. You're trying to change old habits, and that's not going to be easy. If you make up your mind now to go full-out for the next six weeks, to devote some time to Wise Mind Living each day, and to not stop when it gets hard, within a month and a half you will have made a radical difference in your life.

There's no law saying you have to do this in six weeks. It can be intense; for a lot of people, it works best to keep at it over a short horizon. But for others, spreading it out more (though not so much as to lose the thread) will be more effective. You also do not have to master all of this your first time. You can go back to any and all parts of this book as many times as you like, as often as you like. If you get as far as changing your thoughts and find yourself getting bogged down, hang out in that "week" for as long as you need to sort it out for yourself. Or if you get through week six but feel not quite finished, feel free to do the whole thing over again. To get better at all of these Wise Mind Living strategies, you have to practice them. And the more you practice them, the better you'll get. Exactly how you shape that practice time is up to you. You can work with what fits in your life. Keep in mind, though, that the more impossible it seems to fit it in, the more likely you are to really need it!

Any way you go about it, if you want results, you are going to have to put in the effort. It may feel as if I'm asking a lot, with fifteen to twenty minutes a day of mindfulness practice, a daily Wise Mind Review, plus additional assignments each week to hone particular skills. You'll probably need about an hour a day, most days, for all six weeks. But much depends on your perspective: a lot of people fit in an hour a day for a trip to the gym. Or an hour a day watching TV. For the next six weeks, if you are ready to make Wise Mind Living a priority, you can find the time. I promise you, it will pay off.

On your mark . . . get set . . . transform . . .

WEEK 1 GET TO KNOW YOUR EMOTIONS

This first week is all about building awareness of what you are feeling and what you are currently doing (or not doing) about distressing feelings. As discussed in chapter 1, too often you fall into the habit of thinking of it as stress, when what you are really feeling is distressing *emotion*. And you can't do anything about your stress or your distress until you understand, identify, observe, and acknowledge those emotions. Chapters 3, 4, and 5 help with that part of the process. You'll be bringing all of that to bear in this first week, as you uncover the areas of your life that are triggering distress and as you assess how well you are doing with the basic wellness practices that do so much to "distress-proof" you.

Reading Review: Chapters 1, 3, 4, and 5

Wise Mind Living Practices

Checklist: Where Does My Distress Come From? Pinning down the sources of your emotional distress is an essential step. You'll gain awareness of the areas you need to target, which can reveal the potential solutions you need to pursue, including which Wise Mind Living exercises you might want to start with. Put another way: once you know the problem, you'll know which tools you need to make repairs.

Even if you feel stuck in whatever situation you are facing right now, at the very least, identifying it will help you figure out what you can do to best cope with it.

Place an X next to the items that you feel are currently causing you considerable emotional distress:

❑ Conflicts or concerns about your marriage or a relationship

❑ Concerns or worries about your children

❑ Concerns or worries about your parents or other family members

❑ Pressures from other family members or in-laws

❑ Death of a loved one

❑ Health problems or worries (yours or someone else's)

❑ Financial worries

❑ Concerns related to work or career

❑ Long or difficult commute to work

❑ Change in where you are living or will live

❑ Concerns about your current residence

❑ Household responsibilities

❑ Balancing the demands of work and family

❑ Relationships with friends

❑ Limited personal time or time-management pressures

❑ Concerns with your social life

❑ Concerns with your appearance

❑ Boredom

❑ Feelings of loneliness

❑ Worries about growing old

❑ Difficulties with drugs, tobacco, or alcohol

❑ Difficulties with food choices

❑ Other _____

WEEK 1 GET TO KNOW YOUR EMOTIONS

Catch Yourself in Emotion Mind. Becoming more mindful of what you are feeling starts with observing your overall state of mind. You are aiming for Wise Mind, but what you really need to be on the alert for is Emotion Mind, which is just what "Catch Yourself in Emotion Mind" (page 8) is all about. Make this one of your goals every day this week.

Distress-Proofing. Distressing emotions are going to happen no matter what you do. But you can be ready for them and protect yourself from some of their worst effects by taking good care of your physical self. Distressing emotions take a toll on the body, but good health provides a bit of a shield. On the flip side, if you aren't living a healthy lifestyle, you are going to be more vulnerable to the negative effects of distressing emotions.

This week, take time to evaluate your lifestyle choices for what helps and hinders your emotional equilibrium. Assess where you stand on each of five areas: exercise, sleep, diet, time management, and accomplishment. Every day this week, note in your journal when you exercised, whether you ate food that nourished you and kept your blood sugar stable, and how much sleep you got and whether it was restful. You should also track whether you had an alcoholic beverage, smoked, or used nonprescription drugs. Where was your schedule overstuffed or lacking room for important things? How often did you do what felt really fulfilling to you?

At the end of the week, look for patterns (and write them down). What did you do to take care of yourself? Did you do things that aren't helping you? What do you want to do more of? What would you be better off without? Is there anything you want to change? What could you improve—and how?

If you're not up to snuff in any of these areas, make a plan for how you will work yourself toward "snuff." What are you going to do to distress-proof your body? Commit to specific steps—writing them down (hello, Wise Mind Living journal!) is a good way to hold yourself accountable. But don't feel the need to tackle everything at once. You're not going to get perfect overnight (or ever, honestly). Gradual change has a better chance of forming positive new habits, and those have a much better chance of sticking around than do snap or radical changes. Part of your plan should be how to realistically phase whatever you need to accomplish into your life. Once you accomplish whatever plan you write down this week, you can make a new plan for what else you want to do.

Once you have a plan, write down what you will do to keep at it. Monitor your progress. You'll have occasion to pat yourself on the back, which is always good. Besides, putting it on paper increases the odds you'll keep it up. You can document your activity in your journal, but you also have a host of trackers and apps to choose from if you enjoy tech over old-school techniques.

Exercise. Get—or keep—moving. Exercise, in and of itself, helps regulate emotions, actually changing brain chemistry while reducing stress directly and keeping you healthy (and distress resistant). Pretty much any exercise you like—and will do—will fit the bill. A lot of research has been done on cardiovascular exercise, including simple walking programs, but there's also good evidence for the effectiveness of yoga, for example. Pick a form of exercise you are actually likely to do and schedule it into your week. Be realistic! If you won't actually get out of bed at 5 a.m. to hit the gym when the alarm goes off, don't set yourself up to fail. Maybe make a plan to exercise with a friend, as people are more likely to work out when they do it with a partner.

Sleep. Get some rest! A ton of research supports the importance of good sleep habits to both physical health and emotional well-being. (Consider that depriving people of sleep is one form of torture, meant to break someone emotionally.) The average amount of sleep an adult needs to be healthy is seven to eight hours, but you probably know

WEEK 1 GET TO KNOW YOUR EMOTIONS

what amount of sleep feels best for you. Try to get to bed every night this week at a time that allows you to get your optimal amount of sleep.

Healthy Eating. I'm sure I don't have to tell you how important your diet is to your overall health and your body's ability to fight disease, but it might surprise you to hear that dips in blood sugar can dramatically affect your overall mood. Eating small meals every four to five hours and limiting refined carbohydrates (like soda, fruit juice, white bread and pasta, and white rice) can help keep your blood sugar levels stable. Eating lean protein with high-quality carbohydrates (whole grains and vegetables) can also help keep your mood steady. And finally, some very good research suggests that a diet rich in foods with omega-three fats (like wild salmon and sardines) and folic acid (leafy greens and beets) offers some protection against depression and general low mood. So this week, try to be mindful of what and when you are eating. See if you can identify any relationship between your mood and your food.

Time Management. If you are wondering right about now how on earth you are going to squeeze exercise into your schedule, not to mention more *sleep*, then getting a grip on how you spend your time is going to be a really important part of your week. Most of us are overscheduled and running ourselves ragged—and we are more accurate than we know when we say it is making us crazy! Managing your time well is an important way to take care of yourself. It's also the key to finding time to take care of yourself in other ways that you may let slide too often: time to eat a proper meal, time to get a full night's sleep, time to shop for and prepare healthy foods, and time to be social in ways that build strong relationships. So get out your calendar, literally, and make an analysis of how you are spending your time and what does and doesn't serve you. Now, take some stuff off your agenda. It can be done, I swear! Next, put more stuff on the calendar, but only stuff that nurtures you: make sure there's time in your schedule for sleep and exercise (go ahead, write it in there; even give yourself a bedtime if that helps), time to eat right, time for fun, time to do nothing! You can't make more time, but you can carve out the time you have in better ways.

Accomplish Something. Every day, you should try to do at least one thing that makes you feel productive, competent, appreciated, or in control. Something that was a little hard. Something you felt was meaningful or valuable. Something that contributed to your personal growth. You don't need to hit all these areas every time, but touching any of these bases builds your personal reserves of confidence and faith in your ability to handle things when the going gets tough. That's a source of resilience and a coat of armor against distress.

✌ Mindfulness Practice

If You're Happy and You Notice It . . . (page 79). Any mindfulness practice would be good to do this week, but this one is especially nice when you are otherwise thinking about distressing emotions in your life.

✎ Wise Mind Living Journal Assignment

Every day for the next six weeks, you should be writing in your Wise Mind Living journal about what you are feeling and what you are doing about it. This week, you are going to begin with a focus on doing Wise Mind Reviews.

If you haven't designated an official Wise Mind Living journal for yourself, now is the time to do it. You should also establish a regular routine for when you are going to write in your journal. Perhaps you will write every evening at bedtime or each morning as you prepare for the day. The specifics don't matter, as long as you have a standing date with yourself. For this first week of journaling, you'll essentially

WEEK 1 GET TO KNOW YOUR EMOTIONS

track your emotional experience by doing a Wise Mind Review (page 47)—or at least the opening stages of one. You'll fill in the full structure as you go along through the six weeks. This week you're building the foundation.

1. *Jot down which emotions you have this week.* If your label for what you are feeling isn't already one of the Big Eight, you should also include which family of emotions your feeling belongs in: happiness, love, fear, disgust, shame, anger, sadness, or jealousy. (See "Wise Mind Living Practice: Name That Emotion Family," page 57).

   Labeling a distressing emotion can take away some of its power—or at least give you clues about when you are in Emotion Mind. This will let you know that you should not make any decisions just at the moment. So, besides beginning to build a foundation for managing your emotions on this leg of your journey, you may also experience some direct benefit right off the bat. In general, any time you have a distressing emotion during this six-week process, you should take care of it with whatever skills you have on hand. Your repertoire will constantly be expanding, but even here, as you are just starting out, you already have some tools at your disposal, and those are the ones you should use.

2. *Rate each emotion on a scale of zero to ten for intensity.* This is not an exact science: If it's a ten to you, it's a ten. If it seems kind of medium to you, pick a number in the middle of the range. If it's creating no disturbance, you've got yourself a zero.

3. *Any time you rate an emotion higher than five, write down what triggered it.* If you have an eight for anger on Tuesday, what was happening that day? Did you get a bad review from your boss? Get into the same old fight with your teen? Tangle with your mother's nursing home? You may want to reference the "Most Common Types of Prompting Events" list (page 62).

4. *Compare the triggers you identify with the checklist you filled out this week.* They should line up pretty well, but double-check: Is there anything in your journal entries that you want to add to the checklist as an area you have been struggling with but didn't think of at first? Or, for that matter, did you check anything off in the checklist that didn't make an appearance in your journal? You'll want to consider whether this was just a quiet week for that subject in your life or if maybe it isn't a category that really gets your goat that often or that much.

5. *What's your pattern?* After looking at what you think bothers you (from your checklist) and what keeps coming up (from this week's journal), which categories do you need to work on? Is it finances you really need to figure out, or is it a hopeless relationship that's bringing you down? Do you really need a new job or work situation? Should getting a handle on your health be your top priority?

    You should also look for patterns in the specific emotions that make themselves known. Regardless of the trigger, maybe your response is always anger? Maybe you tend toward sadness? Or maybe you've

WEEK 1   GET TO KNOW YOUR EMOTIONS

worked out a pretty good system for handling any feelings of fear, but shame trips you up every time?

As you continue writing in your Wise Mind Living journal over the next six weeks, other kinds of patterns might pop out at you. See if you can find the reasons behind them. Are Wednesdays always bad? Why? Is that, for example, the day your kids stay at their dad's? Or perhaps Wednesdays are always good—maybe thanks to your regular kickboxing class? Do your triggers always involve a certain person: your kids or your folks? Or a theme, such as what you ate, spent, or said? ⚭

WEEK 2 MINDFULNESS

There's nothing more crucial to Wise Mind Living than cultivating mindful awareness. This week of the program is dedicated to practicing controlling your focus, observing your emotions as they are happening, and not getting pulled into the emotion. You'll practice both formally and informally, aiming ultimately to incorporate mindful attention into each moment of your day. You'll also learn to be ready to use mindful attention in times of emotional distress.

Reading Review: Chapter 2

Wise Mind Living Practices

Wise Mind Review: Building Mindful Awareness of Your Emotions.
Complete a Wise Mind Review (page 47) for any distressing emotions you experience each day. For anything that you rate above a five (on the zero-to-ten scale), write about it in your journal and break it down into the component parts of the emotion cycle. You'll expand on this exercise as you move forward, learning additional ways to work with each component. However, for this week, just focus on the following steps: identify and rate the emotion you are experiencing; then write down the prompting event, interpretation, physical response, urge to act, action, and aftereffects. Going through this process, even if you don't do anything else with the information you generate, builds mindful awareness of your emotion.

Mindfulness Practice

You already have a sense of the broad scope of how to practice mindfulness. For beginners, though, it's helpful to start with three basic formal practices: Mindfulness of Breath, Mindfulness of Sound, and Mindfulness Body Scan. As you practice these, you will find that you

WEEK 2 MINDFULNESS

are building a greater ability to hold your focus steady. Once you have achieved greater stability of focus, you will be better able to widen your awareness to include Mindfulness of Thoughts and Feelings and Just This Moment. You're going to do one of these formal practices every day, along with at least one informal practice.

You will continue to practice mindfulness daily throughout this program, and you'll add additional choices for practice as you go. But *this* week, try one of the three most basic formal practices every day. You can keep going through the three as a continuous cycle, one a day. Or after you've tried them all, you can pick whichever one(s) you prefer and stick with those. When you feel a sense of mastery of the three basic practices, you can add the other two into your mix. (If you already began practicing as you read through the first nine chapters of this book, go ahead and include all five formal practices from the outset.) At the same time, choose an informal practice for each day.

As with the journaling, it is helpful to actually schedule appointments for mindfulness practice into your calendar. Formal practice is more suited to scheduling, so you might find planning and tracking informal practices in your journal to be more useful.

THE BASIC THREE

Mindfulness of Breath (page 26)

Mindfulness of Sound (page 28)

Mindfulness Body Scan (page 29)

TWO MORE

Mindfulness of Thoughts and Feelings (page 30)

Just This Moment (page 34)

INFORMAL

Informal Mindfulness 1 (page 31)

Informal Mindfulness 2 (page 32)

✎ Wise Mind Living Journal Assignment

Keep Track of Mindfulness. Make a brief note at the end of each day about whether you practiced mindfulness. You don't have to write detailed notes about your experience (unless you want to), but it will be useful to write down which practice you used as a way of keeping track of how you are progressing in trying each practice.

Look for Patterns. Review your journal entries and look for any themes you see developing, either in the type of prompting event or the predominant emotions you are struggling with. If you see a pattern, you can spend some time to problem-solve the issue or set a goal for how you might handle the situation differently in the future.

Be Mindful of Positives. While you are spending time paying attention to your difficult emotions, give yourself some balance by practicing gratitude as well. Each day, write in your journal something you feel grateful for. There's sometimes surprising power in counting your blessings. ⓪

WEEK 3 ACCEPTANCE AND SELF-SOOTHING

The remaining weeks of this program are devoted to how you can change your emotional experience. But there will also be occasions when you *can't* change. So this week focuses on how to reduce your suffering even when facing emotional pain, which starts with practicing acceptance and extends into strategies for self-soothing.

ᏏᎰ Reading Review: Chapter 9

⑩ Wise Mind Living Practices

This week, you will use each of the following practices at least once. Try to apply one when something distressing comes up. Be sure to also practice when you are *not* right in the middle of the emotion by reflecting on something that's happened in the past or something chronic that keeps coming back around.

Catch Yourself in Nonacceptance (page 137)

Acceptance Meditation (page 140)

Be Kind to Yourself (page 138)

Self-Soothing (page 142)

Lovingkindness: Begin by connecting to your breath. When you are ready, bring to mind someone you love or feel great compassion for. As you think of this person, notice your feelings for him or her as they appear, whether it's a smile spreading across your face or a feeling of warmth in your body.

Now let go of the image of this person from your imagination, keeping your awareness on the feelings of lovingkindness that have arisen.

Now bring to mind someone who supports you, someone who has always been "on your side." Imagine that person facing you. In your mind, wish him or her well by saying:

> May s/he be happy.
>
> May s/he be healthy.
>
> May s/he live in peace.

Next bring to mind a neutral person in your life. Perhaps a stranger that you see often or a person you don't know very well and don't have any strong positive or negative feelings about. Wish that person well using the same words above.

Next, if you feel up to it, try bringing to mind a person for whom you have some conflicted or difficult feelings. Take a moment to consider that this person has the same struggles and needs as all human beings. Use the phrases above to cultivate feelings of lovingkindness for this person.

Finally, bring yourself to mind. See if you can offer lovingkindness to yourself:

> May I be happy.
>
> May I be healthy.
>
> May I live in peace.

See if you can allow yourself to truly feel the sentiment of these words and take them in.

Mindfulness Practices

Formal and Informal Practices. Some of this week's Wise Mind Living practices are mindfulness exercises that you can use as your daily formal practice. Remember to do at least one informal meditation practice every day, too.

Are You Doing It Daily? If you haven't yet committed to doing daily mindfulness practice, take a moment this week to think about

WEEK 3 ACCEPTANCE AND SELF-SOOTHING

what might be getting in the way. Try to problem-solve any of the challenges. Consider scheduling it in your day at a specific time. Relating it to some daily occurrence can be helpful. For example, "Every day when I get home from the office, the first thing I am going to do is ten minutes of mindfulness."

✎ Wise Mind Living Journal Assignment

Wise Mind Review (page 47). Do a Wise Mind Review for any distressing emotion that comes up this week. At the end of the journal entry, add a few notes about what it would mean to practice acceptance of the situation or emotion you are writing about. What would that look or sound or feel like? What would you have to do (or not do) to bring it about? What would you do (or not do) as a result?

What Soothes Me? If you didn't make a list of self-soothing activities that work for you while reading chapter 9, make that a priority this week. If you did make a list but in somewhere other than your Wise Mind Living journal, you might want to transfer it there to keep everything in one place. Just make sure it is easy to reference—maybe inside the back cover if you're using an actual, physical notebook. Review your list to make sure it is fresh in your mind and to make sure you have on hand anything you might need to take advantage of these activities when you need them.

Are You Doing It Daily? Part 2. If you are not already writing every day in your Wise Mind Living journal, recognize that you are halfway through the program and really need to get on the ball with that if you want to reap the benefits. As instructed with mindfulness, think through what might be getting in the way of making a daily commitment, brainstorm solutions to obstacles, and consider holding an official spot in your calendar for journal writing or making it part of an everyday routine. Journal every night before bed, for example. ◍

WEEK 4 CALM YOUR BODY

This week the program shifts to *change* strategies. The work you've done in the first half of the program on awareness, mindfulness, and acceptance has probably already created changes in how you experience your emotions. Starting this week, you'll focus on how to make changes directly, beginning with what is happening in your body.

ᕲ Reading Review: Chapter 6

⦿ Wise Mind Living Practices

Try at least one of the exercises below every day this week. You'll calm your body *and* learn which techniques are the most effective for you. Other forms of relaxation may come in handy as well, such as self-massage and simple stretches, like rolling your head in a half-circle from one shoulder to the other.

Breathe (page 89)

Relax Your Muscles (page 89)

Progressive Relaxation (page 89)

Dive Reflex. Here's a new one for you: as a card-carrying mammal, you have a built-in dive reflex. Besides preparing you to spend some time underwater, it also calms you when you are emotionally overwrought or overwhelmed. It's a nice quick trick to stop any overblown physical reactions in your body—if you know how to trigger it intentionally, that is. The dive reflex protects an animal that spends time underwater (such as an otter or beaver) by forcing the parasympathetic nervous system to kick in. When it does kick in, the effect is calming. Short of a polar bear swim, here's how you make it kick in: fill a sink or bowl

WEEK 4 CALM YOUR BODY

with ice water, bend over it, and put your whole face into it. Hold your breath, of course, and stay there for a count of thirty. You won't believe me until you try it, but this can zap outsized, unpleasant physical symptoms on the spot. This is not for everyday tension. It's for when you are really worked up and acutely aware of physical symptoms of emotion. So give it a whirl.

If it's not possible to actually soak your head, you can get a similar effect by just holding an ice pack to your head and holding your breath.

Mindfulness Practices

Mindfulness Body Scan. This should be your go-to formal practice this week. Do it at least several times over the week. You can choose to either do the traditional mindful practice (not actively trying to change how your body feels—see page 29) or the variation in which you actively calm any parts of your body that are holding your distress (page 91). (Don't forget to do an informal practice as well. There's really no excuse not to, since you can do it while you are getting any other task done.)

Step It Up. Increase the amount of time you are practicing your formal mindfulness meditation. Aim for twenty minutes each time (or five minutes more than you have been doing).

Wise Mind Living Journal Assignment

Before and After. As you practice the relaxation exercises, take note of your overall stress or tension level before you begin and write down the intensity (from zero to ten). Then rate the intensity again after completing the practice. You'll be able to see the progress you're making, and you'll encourage yourself in continuing with the practice. We all need a little positive reinforcement now and then!

Wise Mind Review. Do a Wise Mind Review (page 47) for any distressing emotions. After you have identified what you are feeling in your body, take that as an opportunity to try out one of the body-calming strategies you are concentrating on this week. In your journal, note which strategy you tried. Include the before and after intensity ratings. ⫘

WEEK 5 CHANGE YOUR THOUGHTS

The second category of change strategies you need for Wise Mind Living contains ways to change your thoughts or your thinking.

𝒢𝓇 Reading Review: Chapter 7

⦿ Wise Mind Living Practices

What Was I Thinking? (page 100). Identifying unhelpful thought patterns is a prerequisite for changing them.

Wise Mind Debate (page 104). For any distressing emotions this week, complete a Wise Mind Review, but extend it to do a full-on challenge to your interpretations. You'll probably want to review the list of questions in the Wise Mind Debate exercise for help. Keep going until you have written a more balanced Wise Mind view of the situation.

If you are having a hard time completely believing the Wise Mind view you've come up with, or if this is a recurring theme you've seen in other Wise Mind Review exercises, you can go on to attempt to identify any core beliefs that might be contributing to your strong emotional response. Refer to "Core Beliefs: Is That a Green Banana, or Are You Just Wearing Blue Glasses?" (page 107) for help.

Practice Acceptance. Although the second half of the program moves into change strategies, you should still keep an eye out for opportunities to practice acceptance of the moment. Any time this week you catch yourself not accepting whatever is happening in the moment, stop, relax your body, and try to turn your mind toward acceptance. Remember, acceptance and acknowledgment of distress are the first steps you need to take before you will ever change anything.

✎ Mindfulness Practices

Mindfulness of Thoughts and Feelings (page 30)

Meditate. Using any of the exercises you have already learned, keep up with your daily mindfulness practices—one formal, one informal. Record which practice you do in your journal, along with any notes you want to add.

✎ Wise Mind Living Journal Assignment

Interpretations. This week, your journal entry for any distressing emotion should extend at least through the interpretation section of a Wise Mind Review (page 47).

Patterns. Review your Wise Mind Living journal entries for any problematic thought patterns (see "What Were You Thinking?" page 97) you've identified—as well as any emerging with more, or more recent, entries. ◑

WEEK 6   CHANGE YOUR BEHAVIOR

This week is where the rubber meets the road. In the cycle of emotion, you're coming around to where the cycle finishes. So you'll focus on what action you take in response to your action urges. This is the stuff that may make the biggest obvious difference in your life—the changes you can *see* and that others can see. That's because what you do in the face of one specific experience of emotion carries over to form your behavior in general.

ᕦᕤ Reading Review: Chapter 8

◉ Wise Mind Living Practices

Visualize Yourself Behaving Differently. You can practice changing the knee-jerk reactions that happen when you are in Emotion Mind the same way Olympic divers "see" themselves entering the water with barely a splash before they ever start up the ladder to the board. Take a moment to sit quietly and bring to mind a situation you know is going to be emotionally charged (like confronting your colleague about something he's been slacking on) or a recurring behavior you want to work on changing (like raising your voice when your daughter pushes that button . . . again). Really try to picture the scene as if you were watching it unfold on a movie screen. See yourself pause and count (to yourself) to five before you say anything to your daughter. Imagine yourself calmly explaining the problem and standing your ground as your colleague tries to dismiss your concerns. Try different versions of the scene, refining your responses as you play through the scene to see how it works out. The more you rehearse this way, the more likely you are to "play your part" in real life the next time the situation arises.

Opposite Action (page 128). For any distressing emotion this week, do your very best at acting opposite. Remember, you have to be all-in or it doesn't count (and won't work!).

Problem Solving (page 124). For at least one or two situations that push you into Emotion Mind this week, put Problem Solving into action.

Revaluate Your Distress Proofing. Revisit your actions as far as managing your time, diet, sleep, and exercise for which you set intentions in Week 1. How are you doing with protecting yourself from distress? Review what you've planned and documented in your journal. Create a revised plan for yourself accordingly.

Relax. Check in with how often you are engaging in pleasant activities, and practice relaxation and self-soothing.

Mindfulness Practices

Step It Up. Try increasing the amount of time you are practicing your formal meditation. Aim for twenty minutes each time, or at least five minutes more than you have been doing. Continue your daily informal practice as well. There's really no excuse for not doing the informal practice—you can do it while you are getting any other task done!

Expand Your Focus. Take a moment to appreciate how well you are doing at holding your focus steady, with all the experience you've had by this point. Use the Just This Moment meditation (page 34) at least a couple times this week to flex your focus-control muscle, expanding your focus to include everything that comes into your awareness.

WEEK 6   CHANGE YOUR BEHAVIOR

Observe Your Actions. During your daily formal practice (using Just This Moment and whichever other practices you have liked best over the previous five weeks), pay particular attention to any urges to act that you have as you practice. This might include the desire to move your body, the urge to distract or move your attention away from a place of tension or discomfort, an urge to follow a stream of thought, or even the urge to stop the meditation altogether. This is a chance to practice observing your action urges in real time when you are already calm and focused.

✎ Wise Mind Living Journal Assignment

Wise Mind Review (page 47). Do a Wise Mind Review for any distressing emotions this week, with particular focus on the action urges and action sections. Note what you felt, what you wanted to do, and what you did. Then take it a step further by writing about how you used Opposite Action (page 128) or Problem Solving (page 124).

Revise Your Distress-Proofing Plan. Whatever you discover as you review your progress at distress-proofing your body, revise your plan accordingly. And do it in writing. Remember, regularly including these things in your journal can be a helpful way of keeping yourself motivated. ◍

HAVE TOOL KIT, WILL TRAVEL

Now you've collected all the tools you need. It will take ongoing practice to keep them properly honed and ready for action—anything from doing the whole program over again to periodically revisiting the most useful ideas and exercises to daily use of mindfulness. But you are ready to go out there and experience Wise Mind Living. If you fall off the wagon (actually, *when* you fall off the wagon), just get back on. You're living in Wise Mind, so you know to approach any such stumbles nonjudgmentally.

Just like the journey thus far, your continuing quest won't always be easy. But it will always be worth it.

"Too often people think that emotions just happen to them, but that's not true. When you pay attention to your emotions and know what you're feeling, you will discover that you have a choice about how you feel. Creating the space to mindfully reflect and respond to a situation from the deeper wisdom that comes from balancing emotion and logic—*that is Wise Mind Living*."

DR. ERIN OLIVO

About the Author

Erin Olivo, PhD, MPH, is a licensed clinical psychologist with more than nineteen years of experience treating patients. In addition, she is an assistant clinical professor of medical psychology at Columbia University's College of Physicians and Surgeons. She was formerly the Director of the Columbia Integrative Medicine Program, which she headed in collaboration with Dr. Mehmet Oz.

Dr. Olivo currently maintains a private psychotherapy practice in Manhattan where she works with adults and teenagers who are experiencing difficulties dealing with stress, depression, anxiety, unhealthy relationships, chronic illness, or problems such as self-destructive behavior, addictions, and overeating.

Her treatment approach is solution-focused and integrates cognitive behavior therapy and dialectical behavior therapy with mind-body strategies such as mindfulness meditation. She teaches her patients how to regulate their emotions, tolerate and manage stress, and achieve a more balanced approach to life that she calls Wise Mind Living.

Erin lives in New York City with her husband, Adam, and son, Grady. Visit her website at ErinOlivo.com.

About Sounds True

Sounds True is a multimedia publisher whose mission is to inspire and support personal transformation and spiritual awakening. Founded in 1985 and located in Boulder, Colorado, we work with many of the leading spiritual teachers, thinkers, healers, and visionary artists of our time. We strive with every title to preserve the essential "living wisdom" of the author or artist. It is our goal to create products that not only provide information to a reader or listener, but that also embody the quality of a wisdom transmission.

For those seeking genuine transformation, Sounds True is your trusted partner. At SoundsTrue.com you will find a wealth of free resources to support your journey, including exclusive weekly audio interviews, free downloads, interactive learning tools, and other special savings on all our titles.

To learn more, please visit SoundsTrue.com/bonus/free_gifts or call us toll free at 800-333-9185.

SOUNDS TRUE
many voices, one journey